W9-BTP-653

The Films of Federico Fellini

The Films of Federico Fellini examines the career of one of Italy's most renowned filmmakers through close analysis of five master-pieces that span his career: *La strada, La dolce vita, 8 ½, Amarcord,* and *Intervista.* Providing an overview of Fellini's early career as a cartoonist and scriptwriter for neorealist directors such as Roberto Rossellini, this study traces the development of Fellini's unique and personal cinematic vision as it transcends Italian neo-realism. Rejecting an overtly ideological approach to Fellini's cinema, Bondanella emphasizes the director's interest in fantasy, the irrational, and individualism.

Peter Bondanella is Distinguished Professor of Comparative Liter-ature, Film Studies, Italian, and West European Studies at Indiana University. He is the author of numerous books and articles on Italian cinema, including *The Films of Roberto Rossellini* and *Ital-ian Cinema: From Neorealism to the Present.*

CAMBRIDGE FILM CLASSICS

General Editor: **Ray Carney, Boston University**

The Cambridge Film Classics series provides a forum for revisionist studies of the classic works of the cinematic canon from the perspective of the "new auterism," which recognizes that films emerge from a complex interaction of bureaucratic, technological, intellectual, cultural, and personal forces. The series consists of concise, cutting-edge reassessments of the canonical works of film study, written by innovative scholars and critics. Each volume provides a general introduction to the life and work of a particular director, followed by critical essays on several of the director's most important films.

Other Books in the Series:

Peter Bondanella, *The Films of Roberto Rossellini*
Peter Brunette, *The Films of Michelangelo Antonioni*
Ray Carney, *The Films of John Cassavetes*
Ray Carney and Leonard Quart, *The Films of Mike Leigh*
Sam B. Girgus, *The Films of Woody Allen*
Robert Phillip Kolker and Peter Beicken, *The Films of Wim Wenders*
Amy Lawrence, *The Films of Peter Greenaway*
Scott MacDonald, *Avant-Garde Film*
James Naremore, *The Films of Vincente Minnelli*
James Palmer and Michael Riley, *The Films of Joseph Losey*
Scott Simmon, *The Films of D. W. Griffith*
David Sterritt, *The Films of Alfred Hitchcock*
David Sterritt, *The Films of Jean-Luc Godard*
Maurice Yacowar, *The Films of Paul Morrissey*

The Films of
Federico Fellini

Peter Bondanella
Indiana University

CAMBRIDGE
UNIVERSITY PRESS

PUBLISHED BY THE PRESS SYNDICATE OF THE UNIVERSITY OF CAMBRIDGE
The Pitt Building, Trumpington Street, Cambridge, United Kingdom

CAMBRIDGE UNIVERSITY PRESS
The Edinburgh Building, Cambridge CB2 2RU, UK
40 West 20th Street, New York, NY 10011-4211, USA
477 Williamstown Road, Port Melbourne, VIC 3207, Australia
Ruiz de Alarcón 13, 28014 Madrid, Spain
Dock House, The Waterfront, Cape Town 8001, South Africa

http://www.cambridge.org

© Peter Bondanella 2002

This book is in copyright. Subject to statutory exception
and to the provisions of relevant collective licensing agreements,
no reproduction of any part may take place without
the written perrnission of Cambridge University Press.

First published 2002

Typeface Sabon 10/13.5 pt.   *System* QuarkXpress®   [MG]

A catalog record for this book is available from the British Library

Library of Congress Cataloging-in-Publication Data
Bondanella, Peter E., 1943–
The films of Federico Fellini /Peter Bondanella.
p.   cm. – (Cambridge film classics)
Includes bibliographical references and index.
ISBN 0 521 57325 4 – ISBN 0 521 57573 7 (pb.)
1. Fellini, Federico – Criticism and interpretation.   I. Title.   II. Series.
PN1998.3.F45 B665 2001
791.43′0233′092–DC21
2001035147

ISBN 0 521 57325 4   hardback
ISBN 0 521 57573 7   paperback

Transferred to digital printing 2004

ACC Library Services
Austin, Texas

For Dante and Gianluca

Contents

Illustrations

xiii

Introduction

The Films of Federico Fellini provides an introductory overview of the
Italian director's life and work, with particular focus upon five important films: *La strada, La dolce vita, 8 ½, Amarcord,* and *Intervista.*
The first four works were incredibly successful, both critically and com-
mercially, winning numerous awards and establishing Fellini's international reputation as Italy's most important film director. The last work,
Fellini's penultimate film, provides a summary of Fellini's cinematic
universe and analyzes the nature of cinema itself.

The series in which this book appears – Cambridge Film Classics,
under the general editorship of Ray Carney – aims at providing "a forum for revisionist studies of the classic works of the cinematic canon
from the perspective of the 'new auteurism,' which recognizes that films
emerge from a complex interaction" of various forces and are not only
the result of a director's genius. I accept and even embrace the correc-
tives supplied to auteur criticism, which underline the importance of
economic, political, cultural, bureaucratic, and technical factors in addition to the influence of the creative director. However, in the case of
Federico Fellini, we have the archetypal case of the "art film" director.
Indeed, the very name Fellini has come to stand for the art film itself
and for the kind of creative genius that produced this phenomenon, so
crucial a part of the film culture of the 1960s and 1970s. Inevitably,
the critical pendulum would swing in the opposite direction, since au-

I

teur critics celebrated the director as superstar, concentrating upon such figures as Antonioni, Bergman, Buñuel, Fellini, Hitchcock, and Welles.

Much contemporary film criticism emphasizes a sociological or psychological explanation of cinema and is suspicious of any statements about "original genius." Many who write on the cinema ignore its aesthetic qualities and even refuse to describe or evaluate a work as a "masterpiece." I do not share these prejudices. Moreover, I believe that film historians and critics have an obligation not only to understand the development of this uniquely modern art form but also to assist in the formulation of better taste among filmgoers. Notions of gender, race, class, and culture (understood as a superstructure reflection of class or power relationships, one of the few Marxist ideas that still retains great credibility among academic film critics) have often replaced aesthetic criteria in the literature. Almost no respectable film critic is willing to discuss the emotional appeal of a film because a Brechtian aesthetics – so popular among the followers of Godard and company, or their acolytes in the academy practicing cultural studies – holds incorrectly that when a film appeals to the emotions, it must, of necessity, employ emotional appeal as an ideological sham. In fact, few critics or historians remain concerned with appreciating a film as either a cleverly told story or a beautifully crafted series of visual images. Gender, race, class, and the other sociological flavors of the moment are seen as the dominant critical categories of value, with much else of interest either ignored or ridiculed.

So what is the scholar to do with the cinema of Federico Fellini? His films represent a series of complex chapters in the creation of a unique, private, and personal world of poetic, lyrical, visual images. Fellini stands in complete contrast to the prevailing conventional wisdom of the academy, for if his cinema represents any ideological stand, it is a courageous defense of the imagination as a valid category of knowing and understanding and a rejection of "group thought," political correctness, or sociological explanations of art in favor of the individual imagination and the personal creative act. It is, of course, a truism that film is a collaborative business; but there are collaborations of entirely different kinds. Nothing could be further from Hollywood industrial practice than the manner in which Fellini continued to work throughout his career. His cinema might better be compared to the art produced in the workshop of a Renaissance painter, such as Titian or Michelangelo, than to an industrial product. Every one of Fellini's films was scripted personally by the director, assisted by a very small group of his trusted collaborators whose sensibilities were similar or complementary to Fellini's. These included Tullio Pinelli, Ennio Flaiano, Brunello Rondi, Tonino Guerra, Bernardino Zapponi, and Gianfranco Angelucci. Virtually every detail – costumes, makeup, lighting, sets – of every film was minutely sketched out by Fellini with his famous felt-tip-marker drawings that were then given to each of his collaborators to underline exactly how the Maestro wished a detail to be constructed visually. Nino Rota contributed the sound tracks for his works from his first film through 1979; after his death, Rota was replaced by Luis Bacalov, Gianfranco Plenizio, and Nicola Piovani. Fellini worked with a small group of great cameramen: Otello Martelli, Gianni di Venanzo, Giuseppe Rotunno, Pasquale De Santis, Dario Di Palma, and Tonino Delli Colli. The list could be continued for each category of Fellini's productions: editing (Leo Catozzo, Ruggero Mastroianni, Nino Baragli) and set design (Piero Gherardi, Donato Donati, Dante Ferretti). More than just professional colleagues, Fellini's collaborators were friends of long standing as well as consummate professionals, but the atmosphere on a Fellini set (as chronicled in a large number of publications devoted to Fellini's actual work practices) was always one of adventure, discovery, innovation, and creative improvisation.

Many of his best works took shape in the studios of Cinecittà (especially the famous Teatro 5, the largest studio in Europe). There, Fellini could control everything – light in particular – unlike the less predictable real locations preferred by the neorealists with whom Fellini learned his trade.

Fellini has frequently compared his set to an ocean voyage like that of Columbus toward the New World: The crew constantly attempts to turn back but the director-captain must somehow lead them all to a successful landing. Once again, the model of the Renaissance artists' *bottega* or workshop provides a more suggestive image for the personal creativity associated with Fellini's cinema than the industrialized production methods typical of the contemporary Hollywood studio. We know, for example, that many of Titian's great canvases bear the mark of many shop assistants and apprentices, but the grand overarching design and the most important parts of the canvas were reserved for the master's hand, who was also the workshop manager, and whose genius guided the others. A Titian painting is no less a Titian because of the contributions of his assistants. In like manner, a Fellini film is as close to being the reflection of a single personality as one can come in the industrial art form that is the cinema. None of Fellini's collaborators has ever claimed that any of his films were not ultimately the reflection of a single artist, Federico Fellini. Their collaboration was almost entirely aimed at helping Fellini arrive at the expression of his own visual fantasies. It would be fair to say that if there is a outer limit to the power of the auteur, Fellini certain approached it and even stretched it significantly in comparison to other directors of the postwar period.

In spite of the attempts of academic film critics to marginalize his works because of their supposedly deficient levels of politically correct ideas about women or life in general, Fellini continues to enjoy a healthy respect among serious moviegoers as well as those who actually work in the international film industry. Fellini was a consummate showman, not only an artistic genius but also a master magician and even something of a con man. He was a believer in the power of illusion and prestidigitation, an artist who preferred artifice to reality, and a man who believed that dreams were the most honest expression possible for a human being.

In a revealing conversation with the creator of a BBC documentary on his life and work entitled *Real Dreams: Into the Dark with Federico Fellini,* the director recounted how he was often asked by taxi drivers in Rome, with a bit of embarrassment, why he insisted – as they believed – in making films in which "you can't understand anything": "Ma perché, Signor Fellini, lei fà dei film dove non ci si capisce niente?" ("But, Signor Fellini, why do you make films where nobody understands anything?") Far from being insulted, Fellini valued such an honest (if naïve) question, since it revealed something of importance about the purpose of his work. Thinking back on the question, he said to the BBC journalist:

> It is understandable that when one is so sincere, little is understood. . . . It is a lie that is clear. Everybody understands a lie. But the truth or sincerity pronounced without ideological protections – and therefore other lies – is extremely difficult to grasp. When a man speaks honestly, sincerely about himself, I believe he truly presents himself in his most complex, contradictory, and, therefore, most ambiguous attitude.[1]

It would be difficult to find a statement designed to infuriate contemporary film critics more than Fellini's belief that an artist can speak sincerely and directly to a spectator of a film and that the film, considered foremost as a work of art, represents primarily a moment of artistic expression that establishes a mysterious relationship between storyteller (Fellini) and viewer (the public). The visual images narrating the director's story are ultimately derived from the director's dream life. Rather than ideological pronouncements, Fellini's images typically aim at the communication of emotions or sentiments rather than ideological statements. Fellini honestly (some would say, naïvely) believed that one human being can communicate something of significance to another, without ideological interference. Much of contemporary film criticism is premised on the assumption that such a thing is impossible.[2]

With an artist of Fellini's stature, the moments of intense emotional communication his films inspire in their viewers more than justify their study and continuous rescreening. There are images in a work by Fellini that cannot be reproduced by any other filmmaker and are so clearly a product of a single style and a unique sensibility that they could never be mistaken for the style of any other director. Some of these include Zampanò's single tear on the beach at the conclusion of *La strada* when he realizes that Gelsomina will never return; the magic moment when Marcello Mastroianni and Anita Ekberg enter Rome's Trevi Fountain in *La dolce vita;* the mysteriously festive circle of artistic creativity that concludes *8 1/2* after the director Guido Anselmi has concluded his film must end because he has nothing to say; the unforgettable appearance of the patently cardboard ocean liner *Rex* in *Amarcord;* and Casanova's dream of a waltz with a wooden doll (the only woman with whom he has had a successful sexual liaison) upon a frozen Venetian lagoon. The list of such sublime epiphanies in Fellini's cinema could be lengthened, but the point is simple. No other Italian director, and perhaps no other director in the history of the cinema, has relied so much upon his own private resources to communicate with us through what he hopes will be universal images, images that awaken in us something that is, in the Jungian sense, archetypal. Besides being a storyteller, Fellini was essentially a poet. He created his visual images primarily through an examination of his own dream life, and when his personal expression succeeded in tapping into a similar visual experience in his audience, this linkage, this reception of a personal form of poetic communication, created a powerful emotional experience that is often unforgettable.

If Fellini's attempts to delve into the depths of the human imagination may explain his impact upon individual filmgoers, Fellini's obsession with the irrational is also the aspect of his fantasy that frightens most film critics, whose task is normally to explain rather than to argue (as Fellini himself often asserts) that rational explanations are fruitless. It is this dilemma that a Fellini critic must face squarely: how to apply rational and critical discourse to a cinema that fundamentally privileges fantasy, imagination, and the irrational. I trust that the reader will judge my attempt to do so suggestive and even provocative.

I

Federico Fellini

A Life in Cinema

When Federico Fellini died on 31 October 1993, he had reached the pinnacle of international success. In April of that year, the American Academy of Motion Pictures and Sciences had honored him with a lifetime achievement, an Honorary Award for his entire career. This was his fifth Oscar, after earlier awards in the category of Best Foreign Film for *La strada* (1954), *Le notti di Cabiria* (*The Nights of Cabiria*, 1957), *8½* (1963), and *Amarcord* (1973), not to mention numerous nominations and awards in the technical categories for a number of films.[1] Similar lifetime-achievement awards had earlier been given to Fellini in 1974 by the Cannes Film Festival, and in 1985 by both the Venice Biennale and the Film Society of Lincoln Center. On Broadway, Fellini films inspired important musicals: The Bob Fosse–directed *Sweet Charity* (1965; film 1969) was based upon *Le notti di Cabiria*, whereas Fosse's *Nine* (1981) and earlier film *All That Jazz* (1979) both owed their origins to Fellini's masterpiece, *8½*. References to Fellini or direct citations of his work are found in a wide variety of films by very different directors: Lina Wertmüller's *Pasqualino Settebellezze* (*Seven Beauties*, 1976), Woody Allen's *Stardust Memories* (1980) or *The Purple Rose of Cairo* (1985), Giuseppe Tornatore's *Nuovo Cinema Paradiso* (*Cinema Paradiso*, 1988) and *L'uomo delle stelle* (*The Star Maker*, 1996), or Joel Shumacher's *Falling Down* (1993). Television commercials for various products have frequently employed parodies of Fellini's style.

7

In 1992, a *Sight and Sound* poll asked two groups of individuals for their estimations of which film directors and which films represented the most important creative artists or artistic works during the century-old history of the cinema. The group comprising international film directors or working professionals in the business ranked Fellini first in importance in the history of the cinema, setting him even before Orson Welles by a slim margin of votes.[2] These directors, including such luminaries as Francis Ford Coppola and Martin Scorsese, also indicated they considered *8 1/2* one of the ten most important films made during the past hundred years.

The blockbuster impact of a single Fellini film in 1959 – *La dolce vita* – gave birth to new expressions or vocabulary. In Europe, the aesthetic impact of *La dolce vita* may be accurately compared to the impact of *Gone with the Wind* or *The Godfather* upon American culture. The title itself became identified abroad with the bittersweet life of high society, while in Italy, *dolce vita* came to mean turtleneck sweater, since this kind of garment was popularized by the film. The name of one of the film's protagonists (Paparazzo) gave birth to the English word "paparazzi," which came to mean unscrupulous photographers who snap candid but embarrassing shots of celebrities for the tabloids. Finally, the adjective "Fellinian" became synonymous with any kind of extravagant, fanciful, even baroque image in the cinema and in art in general. More than just a film director, Federico Fellini had become synonymous in the popular imagination in Italy and abroad with the figure of the Promethean creative artist. Like Picasso, Fellini's role as the embodiment of fantasy and the imagination for a generation of fans and film historians transcended his art: People who had never seen one of his films would nevertheless eventually come to recognize his name all over the world and to identify it with that special talent for creating unforgettable images that is at the heart of filmmaking.

Early Days in Rimini and the Romagna

Nothing in Fellini's early life or background would lead the casual observer to predict the heights to which his fame would reach. His parents, Ida Barbiani (a housewife) and Urbano Fellini (a traveling salesman) were of no great distinction in terms of wealth or birth. Fellini was part of a relatively small family by Italian standards of the period:

a younger brother Riccardo was born in 1921, followed by his sister Maddalena in 1929. Fellini himself was born on 20 January 1920 in Rimini, a small town on the Adriatic coast of Italy in a location known best as a watering hole for rich foreign tourists who would frequent the Grand Hotel and other beach establishments during the tourist season, then abandon the sleepy city to its provincial rhythms. Like all vacation towns, Rimini enjoyed a lazy, cyclic existence that alternated between frenetic activity during the tourist season and endless boredom afterward. In an essay entitled "Il mio paese," first published with a beautiful photo album of scenes from his native city and translated into English as "Rimini, My Home Town," Fellini looked back at his origins and concluded that in his life, Rimini represented not an objective fact but, rather, "a dimension of my memory, and nothing more . . . a dimension of my memory (among other things an invented, adulterated, second-hand sort of memory) on which I have speculated so much that it has produced a kind of embarrassment in me."[3] During the entire course of Fellini's career, the director's recollections of his childhood and his adolescence would serve him as an almost inexhaustible source of fertile ideas for his films. The sleepy provincial atmosphere of Rimini was re-created by him for *I vitelloni* (1953) on the opposite side of Italy at Ostia, Rome's ancient seaport. The dream palace of Rimini's Grand Hotel that figures prominently in *Amarcord* as the locus of the frustrated sexual desires of the entire male population of Rimini stands as one of the most unforgettable images in all of Fellini's works. Even the distant destination of the grand metropolis of Rome toward which all Fellini's anxious provincials are drawn, a theme that figures prominently in so many of his films and particularly in *La dolce vita* or *Roma* (*Fellini's Roma*, 1972), must always be read against the background of Rimini.[4]

Other provincial influences were also subtly at work during Fellini's early childhood. Fellini regularly was taken to the tiny town of Gambettola in the inland area of Romagna. There Fellini visited his grandmother, encountered the typical kind of eccentric figures that rural life in Italy has always spawned, including a frightening castrator of pigs, numerous gypsies, witches, and various itinerant workers. The mysterious capacity of many of Fellini's film characters (in particular, Gelsomina of *La strada*) to enjoy a special relationship with nature surrounding them was directly inspired by Fellini's childhood visits to his grandmother's home. Gambettola seems to have been a breeding ground for characters with diminished mental capacities but with special emotional qualities, and in *La voce della luna* (*The Voice of the Moon*, 1990), Fellini's last film, he creates another Gelsomina-like figure (Ivo) who seems to be a half-wit but who enjoys an emotional depth that normal characters cannot fathom or imitate.[5] The famous harem sequence of *8 1/2* where a young Guido is bathed in wine vats before being sent to bed is only one of the many scenes from Fellini's cinema that recall his childhood past in Gambettola. However important Rimini, Gambettola, and the Romagna were to Fellini's nostalgic memories of his childhood, there were other more formative cultural influences taking place there that would begin to shape his early career. As a child, the young Federico was well known for his unusual imagination: He was a precocious sketch artist and spent hours playing with a tiny puppet theater. His favorite reading materials were the comic strips that appeared in an extremely popular magazine for children, *Il corriere dei piccoli*, which, as early as 1908 in Italy, reproduced the traditional American cartoons drawn by such early American artists as Frederick Burr Opper (1857–1937), Billy De Beck (1890–1942), Winsor McCay (1869–1934), George McManus (1884–1954), and others. Opper's *Happy Hooligan* (called *Fortunello* in Italy) is the visual forerunner not only of Charlie Chaplin's Little Tramp but also of Gelsomina in *La strada*, Fellini's most famous creation, as well as Cabiria in *Le notti di Cabiria*. Winsor McCay's *Little Nemo in Slumberland*, a wonderfully drawn strip about a little boy who goes to bed and experiences fantastic dreams, was certainly a powerful influence upon Fellini, whose visual style in several films (*Satyricon* [*Fellini Satyricon*, 1969] and *I clowns* [*The Clowns*, 1970], in particular) would recall McCay's character Little Nemo. Years later, when Fellini began to analyze his own dreams under the influence of a Jungian psychologist, he would begin a series of drawings in his dream notebooks that utilize the style of the early American comic strip, and he would even dream of himself as a young boy in the same sailor-suit costume worn by Little Nemo in McCay's strip.[6] Even though the cartoon characters created by Walt Disney (1901–66) in both the comic strips and the films ultimately became far more popular in postwar Italy than were these early artists' characters in the newspapers for children, Fellini's own visual style, particularly in his preparatory drawings or his dream notebooks, always remained wedded to the early comic-strip style, not the Disney variety.

In 1937, Fellini published his first drawings in a magazine issued by the Opera Balilla, the Fascist youth organization. These were caricatures of his friends from a camping trip from the summer of 1936. During the 1937 vacation season, Fellini joined forces with a friend named Demos Bonini to set up a sketch and caricature shop called FEBO that sold such humorous sketches to summer tourists, and during the same year, Fellini drew caricatures of famous European or American actors to be displayed by the owner of Rimini's movie theater, the Fulgor (another mythical site immortalized by *Amarcord*). Some of these sketches are still extant and may be examined in the catalog of the first retrospective on Fellini held in Rome in 1995, soon after his death.[7] Fellini would soon send his drawings, accompanied by one-liners, to the *Domenica del corriere*, where a number of them were published between 1938 and 1939, when he left Rimini for Rome. Before leaving Rimini, Fellini also encountered the caricaturist Giuseppe Zanini, internationally famous as Nino Za, who had made a fortune publishing humorous sketches of the world's great actors and actresses in Germany. Za's artistic style, like that of the early American comics, would become another formative influence upon Fellini's drawings.[8] Before moving to the capital, during a six-month period between 1937 and 1938, Fellini went to Florence and presented himself at the editorial office of the weekly humor magazine 420, then managed by Mario Nerbini. There, if we may believe one of Fellini's possibly apocryphal accounts,[9] Fellini and another sketch artist named Giove Toppi created a substitute for the popular cartoon strip *Flash Gordon* by Alexander Raymond (1909–56), which the Fascist government found insufficiently Italian. Whether or not this story is a true one, years later, in shooting *Satyricon*, Fellini noted that he attempted in the film to re-create some of the particular colors typical of the comic strips of the time, including those by Raymond.[10]

The Move to Rome and Fellini's Precinematic Career as a Writer

In 1939, the young Fellini moved to Rome with his mother and sister. In Rome, he enrolled in the Faculty of Law at the university but never completed a degree. Soon, the friends Fellini met would play a determinative role in the choice of his eventual career as cartoonist, journalist, gagman, and scriptwriter. Fellini began to work on *Marc'Aurelio,* a widely distributed and highly influential biweekly humor magazine filled with gags, cartoons, and brief comic sketches. Between 1939 and the end of November 1942 (the date of Fellini's last contribution to the magazine), Fellini's work included more than two thousand pages of text – cartoons, gags, comic columns.[11] The *Marc'Aurelio* experience also inspired Fellini's first book, a small pamphlet probably published in 1942 (there is no publication date on the title page) under the title *Il mio amico Pasqualino* [My Friend Pasqualino]. It contains numerous drawings that attest to the influence of the comic-strip style of Opper: Pasqualino bears a clear physical resemblance to Happy Hooligan. Perhaps even more intriguing is the possibility that the content of this book may well reflect Fellini's early reading of Franz Kafka, a writer practically unknown in Italy at the time.[12]

The staff of *Marc'Aurelio* was filled with writers whose contribution to the Italian cinema would soon become legendary. They would eventually include Cesare Zavattini (the scriptwriter for Vittorio De Sica's neorealist classics); Ruggero Maccari (who would introduce Fellini to key figures in the cinema, such as the actor Aldo Fabrizi); Ettore Scola (the future director); and Bernardino Zapponi (who would eventually become one of Fellini's major scriptwriters in the 1960s and 1970s). Some of Fellini's friends in Rome did not have a connection to *Marc'Aurelio,* such as the painter Rinaldo Geleng (who became his lifelong friend and who would assist him as set decorator in a number of his films) or Nino Za, who was working in the capital at the time and who did a caricature of a young and very impoverished Fellini that the director kept on his office desk until his death.[13] Still, the brief period of work at *Marc'Aurelio* would be the determining moment in Fellini's life, for the writers, gagmen, and scriptwriters whom he met on the editorial board, who were almost all simultaneously writing for the cinema in some capacity, provided the same kind of entry into the world of show business that a young student today might well find in a film school in Los Angeles or New York.

Fellini immediately fell in with a crowd of actors and vaudeville players. As has always been the case in the cinema, connections and

Nino Za's sketch of Fellini (1942), a drawing that remained on Fellini's desk until his death. [*Photo:* Federico Fellini]

being at the right place at the right time (in addition to talent) make a difference. Maccari introduced Fellini to Aldo Fabrizi, the actor soon to become world famous as the partisan priest in Roberto Rossellini's *Roma, città aperta* (*Open City,* 1945). Fabrizi would eventually present Fellini to Rossellini. Between the end of Fellini's collaboration on *Marc'Aurelio* and his collaboration with Rossellini as the scriptwriter on *Roma, città aperta,* which launched his international fame with his first nomination for an Oscar in the category of scriptwriting, Fellini had to survive the war and the occupation. Some accounts of Fellini's first activity behind a camera date it from 1943, when he was dispatched to Tripoli to work on a film directed by Gino Talamo entitled *Gli ultimi Tuareg* [The Last Tauregs]. The on-location shooting was cut short by the Allied invasion of North Africa, and just before Tripoli fell to the Allied troops, Fellini managed to obtain a seat on one of the last German transport planes leaving the area.[14] Returning, he worked on a number of scripts for minor films. In 1943, he married Giulietta Masina, a theatrical actress employed by the EIAR (Ente Italiano Audizioni Radiofoniche, the state-owned radio service). After the liberation of Rome on 4 June 1944, Fellini maintained his family by drawing portraits and caricature sketches for Allied soldiers at The Funny Face Shop, a store he opened on the Via Nazionale.

There is no doubt that Fellini's film career was launched in style with the international success of Rossellini's melodramatic account of wartorn Rome. Fellini was responsible for much of the success of the film, being principally concerned with creating the character of the partisan priest, played by his friend Fabrizi. Since *Roma, città aperta* not only launched the international film careers of Roberto Rossellini and Federico Fellini but also announced to the world the birth of what film historians and critics would label Italian *neorealism,* much of Fellini's early career would involve a slow but persistent evolution toward an entirely different kind of cinema than that embodied in either *Roma, città aperta* or *Paisà.* Italian neorealism may be briefly (but superficially) defined as a film style favoring documentary effects, real locations (as opposed to the so-called artificiality of studios), natural lighting, nonprofessional actors, and a progressive (if not leftist) political stance treating contemporary social problems (unemployment, the war, the partisan struggle, old age, strikes, the working class, etc.).[15] When Fellini's film career began almost immediately to diverge from this kind

On location during the shooting of the monastery sequence of *Paisà*: Roberto Rossellini, a young monk, and an even younger Federico Fellini. [*Photo:* Federico Fellini]

of cinema, he would soon find himself the target of relentless negative criticism from the Left.

Between 1945 and the shooting of his first feature film, *Luci del varietà* (*Variety Lights*, 1950), Fellini contributed an extraordinary amount of work as scriptwriter to the Italian cinema. Besides the scriptwriting for Rossellini's second postwar work, *Paisà* (*Paisan*, 1946), Fellini made substantial contributions to Rossellini's *Il miracolo* (*The Miracle*, 1948), in which Fellini appeared himself for the first time as an actor, playing the mysterious vagabond. The film's controversial treatment of the nature of sainthood was scripted by Fellini primarily as a vehicle for Anna Magnani, then Rossellini's mistress. It offended some conservative Catholics in America and was censored. The distributor ultimately took the case as far as the U.S. Supreme Court, where it would serve as the occasion for the ground-breaking decision delivered on 26 May 1952 in *Burstyn v. Wilson*, which ruled that film was not merely a business but was also a means of expression protected by the First Amendment, reversing a 1915 decision to the contrary. Furthermore, because the state was not charged with protecting specific religions from criticism, the court ruled that sacrilege could not be an excuse for artistic censorship.[16] Thus, Fellini's script and his acting performance had a direct impact upon the making of constitutional law in the United States.

Fellini's scripts for several films by Rossellini, often starring Ingrid Bergman, were expressions of the same kind of Christian humanism that infuriated leftist critics in Fellini's own early works. In addition to *Il miracolo*, Fellini made important contributions to Rossellini's *Francesco, giullare di dio (The Flowers of Saint Francis*, 1950), as well as uncredited work for his *Europa '51* (aka *The Greatest Love*, 1952). Fellini's scripts for pictures produced by the Lux Film company were equally significant in the immediate postwar period. They include *Il delitto di Giovanni Episcopo (Flesh Will Surrender*, 1947), *Senza pietà (Without Pity*, 1948), and *Il mulino del Po (The Mill on the Po*, 1949) for Alberto Lattuada; *Il passatore (A Bullet for Stefano*, 1947) for Duilio Coletti; *In nome della legge (In the Name of the Law*, 1949), *Il cammino della speranza (The Path of Hope*, 1950), and *La città si difende (Four Ways Out*, 1951) for Pietro Germi; and *Persiane chiuse (Behind Closed Shutters*, 1951) for Luigi Comencini. Although Fellini's own career as a director would rely primarily upon his own personal vision of the world, in the studio films his work touched upon traditional American genres (the gangster film, the film noir, the western). So much work on so many important films would represent the bulk of a career for a lesser talent than Fellini; but for the precocious young man fresh from the provinces and eager to make his mark in the world, these major credits represented only the penultimate step toward direction. It is also important to underline the fact that Lux Film was responsible for some of the very best neorealist films produced in the postwar period – not only the key works by Germi and Lattuada above but also such seminal titles as *Riso amaro (Bitter Rice*, 1948) by Giuseppe De Santis and *Senso (Wanton Countessa*, 1954) by Luchino Visconti.

Since one of the most frequent critiques of Fellini's early cinema was that it represented a betrayal of neorealism, it is important to note that Fellini's experiences as a scriptwriter exposed him to two entirely different kinds of director. On the one hand, Roberto Rossellini's practice was as far removed from the industrial system of Hollywood filmmaking as could be imagined. Rossellini's scripts were written and rewritten at the local trattoria shortly before shooting began, there was a constant lack of funding, and work generally moved from one day to the next without any master plan such as was normally required of a capitalist studio intent upon maximizing its profit and minimizing its risks. The precarious nature of such an operation directed by the flamboyant personality of Rossellini was precisely what Fellini loved about working with him. Indeed, even though Fellini would become the most exacting of taskmasters on his own sets at Cinecittà and rarely use authentic locations in his mature work – preferring precisely the so-called artificiality of the studio because it was completely under his artistic control – he would also attempt to re-create the chaotic mood typical of Rossellini's sets during his own shooting in order to be open to intuitive inventions and serendipitous surprises.

On the other hand, it is too often forgotten that Fellini also apprenticed with Lux, a traditional commercial studio company similar in operation and outlook to Hollywood studios, where he became the trusted collaborator of a number of professional directors whose artistic products emerged from exactly the same kind of production company as its Hollywood counterparts. In fact, Fellini remembers that Carlo Ponti and Dino De Laurentiis, then young producers working for Lux (and, later, coproducers for *La strada*), even attempted to mimic the style of Hollywood moguls, displaying three or four telephones on their desks, puffing huge cigars, and propping their feet up on their desks – in perfect imitation of the images of Hollywood producers they had seen on the silver screen.[17]

Thus, when Fellini began his career in the cinema as a director, he had undergone a unique experience: Not only had he entered the active life of scriptwriting through the school of a completely nontraditional director, Rossellini, who enjoyed breaking all of the conventions or rules of the trade; but he was, simultaneously, employed by a production company that was arguably the most advanced expression of industrial capitalism in the Italian movie industry. Both of these lessons would serve Fellini well in the future.

From Neorealist Scriptwriting to Direction: The Trilogy of Character in *Luci del varietà, Lo sceicco bianco,* and *I vitelloni*

While continuing to write scripts for Lux Film, Fellini's debut as a director came about as the result of a collaborative effort with one of Lux's more experienced directors, Alberto Lattuada. The film (starring his own wife, Giulietta Masina, as well as Lattuada's wife, Carla Del Poggio) was entitled *Luci del varietà* (*Variety Lights,* 1950). The film was not a success (ranking sixty-fifth in gross ticket sales in the 1950–1 season) and even failed to garner the usual government subsidy given to works considered of artistic merit; yet its bittersweet depiction of the world of show business and the sometimes tawdry reality behind the illusions on the stage of a traveling vaudeville troupe mark this debut in the cinema as a work with Fellini's personal signature. In fact, a number of the recurrent visual images in Fellini's cinema are exploited in this film: the deserted piazzas at night that Fellini frequently employs to provide an objective correlative for the often superficial illusions of his characters; frenzied nocturnal celebrations followed by the inevitable letdown at dawn; processions of grotesque and unusual characters with amusing physical traits reminiscent of the figures Fellini drew for his cartoons and sketches in *Marc'Aurelio*. Seen in retrospect, *Variety Lights* contains the entire range of the style and thematic concerns of Fellini's early cinema before the watershed appearance of *La dolce vita* in 1959.

This interesting but too infrequently studied film was followed in 1952 by the first film directed solely by Fellini, *Lo sceicco bianco* (*The White Sheik*). Based upon an original idea provided to Fellini's producer, Carlo Ponti, by Michelangelo Antonioni, Fellini collaborated with Tullio Pinelli (1908–) and Ennio Flaiano (1910–72) on the script, beginning a collaboration that would last for many years afterward. Nino Rota, thereafter to be identified almost entirely with Fellini's cinema, also began his lifelong collaboration with Fellini as the creator of a particular brand of music that would become an integral part of the Fellini cinematic experience. *Lo sceicco bianco* represents a hilarious parody of the world of the *fotoromanzo* – the photo-novel or sentimental true-romance-type magazine that sold millions of copies in postwar Italy and boasted such titles as *Grand Hotel* or *Sogno*. Before the advent of mass audiences for television, such pulp magazines filled the

Fellini's directorial debut in *Luci del varietà:* Liliana (Carlo Del Poggio) and Checco (Peppino De Filippo) provide a bittersweet vision of the world of show business. [*Photo:* The Museum of Modern Art/Film Stills Archive]

same role in popular culture that soap operas fill today. They were produced by employing black-and-white photographs (not colored cartoon drawings), while the dialogue was contained within the traditional comic balloon. In *Lo sceicco bianco,* Fellini not only pokes gentle fun at the kind of unsophisticated people who take such publications seriously, but he also implicitly provides a hilarious parody of the film star Rudolph Valentino (1895–1926), the original Latin lover on the silver screen whose brief but meteoric career included several films in which he played a sheik (*The Sheik,* 1921; *Son of the Sheik,* 1926). Fellini's sheik is a much less imposing figure, a character in a *fotoromanzo* played brilliantly by a young Alberto Sordi. Giulietta Masina plays a cameo role as a prostitute named Cabiria, a figure that Fellini will use as the central character in the later masterpiece entitled *Le notti di Cabiria,* also starring Masina.

Ivan Cavalli (Leopoldo Trieste) is chased by a parade of *bersaglieri* troops in *Lo sceicco bianco*, a financial failure now recognized as a comic masterpiece. [*Photo:* The Museum of Modern Art / Film Stills Archive]

Fellini's third film, set in a town obviously based upon his hometown of Rimini on the Adriatic coast, managed to rescue his early career from an undeserved obscurity and critical neglect after the negative reception of his first two works (today considered comic gems). Entitled *I vitelloni* (1953), it was awarded a Silver Lion at the Venice Film Festival by a jury headed by the future Nobel laureate Eugenio Montale. It also first attracted the attention of critics abroad, especially in France and the United States, whose accolades would eventually prove an effective counterweight to the harsh attacks within Italy, from both the Right and the Left, that Fellini would endure throughout his long career. Like the first two films in what I have elsewhere termed the "trilogy of character,"[18] Fellini's third film concentrates upon the illusory dreams of five young men in the provinces: They are all *vitelloni,* a word Fellini recalls from his regional dialect to mean an immature, lazy young man without any clear notion of direction in his life. The five *vitelloni* each harbor a specific dream – to leave for the capital city, to write a great play, to play the local Don Giovanni, and so forth – and the social masks of each are eventually stripped away to reveal the somewhat hollow, superficial reality of their true personalities. Fellini's particular penchant for the world of show business continues in this film, as the moments of crisis during which the flawed personalities of the *vitelloni* come to the surface have some link to the entertainment world – a beauty contest, a carnival, a movie theater, a variety theater performance. At the close of the film, a single character – Moraldo – abandons the provincial backwater where such superficial illusions have trapped the other protagonists in a lotus-land of tawdry dreams and heads for the capital city of Rome. Many critics, especially those of an autobiographical bent, consider Moraldo Fellini's alter ego and the predecessor of Marcello, the journalist from the provinces who becomes the famous protagonist of *La dolce vita.* Moraldo did become the major figure in a script called *Moraldo in città* (*Moraldo in the City*), which was written in 1954 but never realized as a film, although parts of the script later surfaced in *Le notti di Cabiria* and in *La dolce vita.*[19]

Fellini's first three films treat the daydreams and the illusions of provincial Italians who grow up longing to change their lives by moving to the capital or by becoming a famous personage in show business. Even though such content was hardly what film viewers had come to

In Fellini's first commercial success, *I vitelloni*, a drunken Alberto in drag (Alberto Sordi) dances with a carnival reveler. [*Photo:* The Museum of Modern Art / Film Stills Archive]

expect from neorealist cinema, which dealt more immediately and more polemically with such pressing social problems as unemployment, the war, the Resistance, and the postwar economic recovery, it was certainly possible at the time Fellini made his debut to include his early cinema within the rubric of neorealism. After all, the view of provincial life and its bittersweet critique as full of comic illusions and failed characters could easily lend itself to a more politicized critique of Italian bourgeois culture by the Left. What such critics failed to comprehend, in their initial attempts to save Fellini from the charge of betraying neorealism's progressive politics, was that even while Fellini poked gentle fun at the characters he created who tried to make their illusions and dreams a reality, he was nevertheless more interested in the subjective side of life and the power of illusion and fantasy than he was in the so-called objective, materialistic, and ideological issues that occupied so many Italian film critics.

International Fame on the Road beyond Neorealism: *La strada, Il bidone,* and *Le notti di Cabiria*

If Fellini's trilogy of character retained a neorealist flavor in what critics today now praise as the accurate and believable (if comic) portrait of the Italian provinces in the 1950s, Fellini's subsequent trilogy of grace or salvation moved immediately beyond the ideological boundaries of neorealist cinema defined as socially relevant cinema and toward a philosophical position of Christian existentialism that exploited traditional iconography or religious concepts (such as that of conversion) to mark out an entirely different kind of cinema.

Immediately after shooting *I vitelloni*, Fellini shot a single brief episode, *Un'agenzia matrimoniale* ([A Matrimonial Agency], 1953), for *Amore in città* (*Love in the City*), a project conceived by Cesare Zavattini, perhaps the most famous of the neorealist scriptwriters, who wanted to create a new style of cinema comparable to the daily newspaper. Zavattini called this kind of cinematic journalism that would focus upon current events *il film inchiesta* – the film inquiry or investigation. He hoped that by using six different directors (Fellini, Antonioni, Lattuada, Francesco Maselli, Carlo Lizzani, and Dino Risi), all of whom would employ nonprofessional actors to create something like a news magazine, he could keep Italian cinema on what he considered its proper course toward the simple representation of daily life. Fellini's contribution involved a complete overturn of Zavattini's plan, for he proposed a story about a reporter who goes to a marriage agency, posing as a client, to look for a woman willing to marry a werewolf. Apparently, the naïve Zavattini actually believed Fellini's claim that his film was based on a true story. So much for social realism!

Fellini turned in his next three films toward a sharper break with his neorealist heritage than was first apparent in his earlier films. The most important of this trilogy, *La strada* (1954), Fellini once described as "really the complete catalogue of my entire mythical world."[20] *La strada* is a fable about a circus strongman (Zampanò) who takes on a dimwitted girl (Gelsomina) to assist him in his act.[21] He accidentally kills a high-wire artist (Il Matto or the Fool) before her eyes, causing Gelsomina to go mad and forcing Zampanò to abandon her after he has realized, only too late, how much she has changed his brutish, animal-like existence through her mysterious presence. Because *La strada* rests squarely upon a secular form of a major Christian notion – the Catholic belief that a conversion can radically change a person's life – the unprecedented international success of this work also touched off a very interesting debate between warring critical camps in France and Italy that was to continue (but with a reversal of protagonists and intellectual positions) until the appearance of *La dolce vita*.

After *La strada* won for Fellini the Silver Lion at Venice in 1954 and his first Oscar for Best Foreign Film in 1956 (not to mention dozens of other awards), still continuing his interest in the fundamental psychological changes of conversion that would come about from an act of secular grace in ever more complex individuals, Fellini next shot *Il bidone* (1955), casting Broderick Crawford in the leading role of a con man named Augusto who often poses as a priest. *Il bidone* means "the swindle" in Italian, and Fellini had originally thought of Humphrey Bogart for the leading role, but Crawford was perhaps equally as suitable, since he was associated by audiences all over the world with Hollywood gangster pictures. With *Il bidone*, Fellini took a traditional Hollywood genre and gave it a special Fellinian twist, for the plot of the film represents a variation of the Christian story of the good thief, the character near Christ on the cross, and traces Augusto's descent into a personal hell through five days of confidence games and a growing sense of remorse.[22]

The presentation of *Il bidone* at the 1955 Venice Film Festival was a disaster and would prevent Fellini from presenting one of his films at Venice until the opening of *Satyricon* in 1969. Nevertheless, the subsequent *Le notti di Cabiria* (1957), assisted by another brilliant performance by Giulietta Masina as Cabiria Ceccarelli (awarded Best Actress at the Cannes Film Festival for her efforts), enjoyed international acclaim and earned Fellini's second Oscar for Best Foreign Film. Fellini initially had difficulty obtaining backing for this film, which he had in mind even before *Il bidone*, because he wanted to shoot a picture on prostitution at precisely the moment when the question of legalized prostitution had become a burning social issue in Italy. Ultimately legalized prostitution was banned in 1958 by the Merlin Law, finally closing the state-inspected brothels that had played such a large role in the sexual education of every Italian male of Fellini's generation. Although Fellini toyed with the idea of a pseudoneorealist study of prostitution in Italian society – interviewing numerous women in "the life" and even hiring the then little-known Pier Paolo Pasolini to help him with realistic or earthy Roman dialogue that would reflect the milieu in which Cabiria thrives – *Le notti di Cabiria* employs a by-now familiar Fellinesque picaresque plot, ambling around Rome with Cabiria and her friends or acquaintances, to suggest an entirely nonrealistic and essentially illusionistic vision of the world. In fact, the key sequence of the film – a vaudeville act during which Cabiria's dreams and aspirations are revealed to the audience while the plucky prostitute is in a trance – underlines how completely Fellini's cinema has focused upon the irrational, subjective states of his characters and how little Cabiria's socioeconomic status (the focus of any neorealist inquiry into the social aspects of prostitution) matters to the director.

The Mature Auteur: *La dolce vita* and a New Subjective Film Narrative

With the unprecedented international success of *La dolce vita,* Fellini departed in a number of fundamental ways from the aesthetic and thematic preoccupations that had earned him the coveted title of auteur from international critics. Whereas his cinema first emerged in his trilogy of character from a dialectical relationship with neorealist cinema, a style of filmmaking in which Fellini's career began as a scriptwriter, the evolution of Fellini's film language in *La dolce vita* and afterward – most particularly in *8 ½* and *Giulietta degli spiriti* (*Juliet of the Spirits,* 1965) – would move beyond any overriding concern with the representation of social reality and concentrate upon the subjective, often irrational areas of human behavior connected with the psyche or the unconscious. As *La dolce vita* and *8 ½* are the subjects of separate chapters in this study, it is sufficient here to note that the lush fresco of the titular "sweet life" in the first film, presenting a comic panorama of life defined as image and style, broke all Italian box-office records and most of those in Europe as well, winning a number of international awards, including the Grand Jury Prize at Cannes. *La dolce vita* – especially in conjunction with the subsequent *8 ½,* a film about a filmmaker's inability to make his film – resulted in the virtual canonization of Fellini as *the* archetypal genius, the auteur of auteurs, the undisputed king of what is today, in retrospect, referred to as the European "art" film. Finally, and most surprisingly, Fellini found the leftist Italian press in his camp (after years of attacks upon his works for their supposedly Catholic character), while some supporters who had admired the Christian elements in his earlier films now abandoned him. Thousands of tourists would flock to Rome for years to come in search of the Via Veneto locations Fellini had actually created in the huge Teatro 5 at Cinecittà, or to toss a coin into the Trevi Fountain into which Fellini's star, Anita Ekberg, had waded with Marcello Mastroianni. *La dolce vita* marks the first of many close collaborations between Fellini and Italy's greatest actor: Mastroianni, who died in 1996, only a few years after Fellini. Mastroianni eventually became identified in the public's mind as Fellini's alter ego. The picaresque, open narrative forms toward which Fellini's works in the trilogy of character and the trilogy of grace or salvation had been evolving now take center stage in Fellini's style. In *La dolce vita,* Fellini himself spoke of changing the representation of reality in his film in much the same way as the cubist artist Picasso has smashed the traditional painter's obsession with vanishing points and mimesis by deconstructing the reality of material objects into their potential surfaces.[23]

Between *La dolce vita* and *8 1/2,* Fellini made an extremely important film that has not enjoyed much critical attention: *Le tentazioni del Dottor Antonio* (*The Temptations of Doctor Antonio,* 1962), a contribution to an episodic film entitled *Boccaccio '70* to which Luchino Visconti, Mario Monicelli, and Vittorio De Sica made contributions along with Fellini.[24] This brief work, as well as another episode Fellini contributed to yet another film by several hands – *Toby Dammit* (1968) for *Tre passi nel delirio* (*Spirits of the Dead*), shot with Louis Malle and Roger Vadim – are absolutely crucial for an understanding of the evolution of Fellini's style.[25] These episodic films reflect the growing influence of dreams and psychoanalysis upon Fellini, most particularly the theories of Jung. Fellini's interest in dream imagery would continue for the rest of his career. Moreover, Fellini (who had begun his interest in psychoanalysis during his personal crisis that coincided with the shooting of *La strada*) now began to analyze his own dreams by sketching them in large notebooks with vivid felt-tip markers.

The impact of Jungian psychoanalysis upon Fellini is everywhere apparent in *8 1/2* and *Giulietta degli spiriti.* In many respects, the two works are different sides of the same coin – an exploration of the Jungian anima and animus. In the case of *8 1/2*, this exploration takes place within the subjective fantasy world of a film director whose similarity to Fellini himself suggests a close biographical connection. In *Giulietta degli spiriti,* Giulietta Masina plays a housewife who explores her married life and comes to find that she has been living too long in the shadow of her husband. Although criticized by some feminists, *Giulietta degli spiriti* represents Fellini's sustained attempt to understand the female psyche. It is certainly one of the first postwar European films to espouse the cause of women's liberation.

After the completion of *Giulietta degli spiriti,* Fellini intended to film a work tentatively entitled *Il viaggio di G. Mastorna* [The Voyage of G. Mastorna].[26] Originally written during the summer of 1965 with Dino Buzzati (1906–72), the enigmatic Italian writer of mysterious short stories who was often called the Italian Franz Kafka, the film was plagued by numerous problems. The usual arguments with reluctant producers that characterized most of Fellini's previous creations now took second place to his serious physical collapse caused by the rare Sanarelli–Shwartzman syndrome. Fellini's active dream life also entered a crisis, and many of the dreams from this period underline a blockage of artistic inspiration and the impossibility of realizing *Mastorna*. It has been suggested that Fellini felt it impossible to make *Mastorna* because the subject matter of the film was ultimately about the nature of death, and his musician protagonist was too closely identified by the director with himself.

It was specifically as a means of combating a creative mental block connected to the abortive production of *Mastorna,* as well as the physical crisis brought on by his life-threatening illness, that Fellini took a step he always preferred to avoid: He agreed to make a film based upon a literary work not of his own creation. Literature, Fellini always claimed, could at best only provide the cinema with a general narrative plot, since for Fellini the cinema was primarily a visual, not a literary, medium, with light, and not words, as its means of communicating ideas or emotions. Thus, he shot *Toby Dammit* in the episodic film *Tre passi nel delirio* but changed the storyline so drastically that almost only one element of the literary source (the decapitation of the main character after placing a bet with the devil) remained from Edgar Allan Poe's original. In Fellini's version, the protagonist becomes a drug-dazed Shakespearean actor down on his luck who is hired by the Vatican to make a Catholic western (this was the heyday of the Italian spaghetti western made famous by Sergio Leone).

Fellini's next effort was far more significant: a brilliant but highly personal visual extravaganza of lush, baroque imagery that followed in general terms the narrative found in the classic prose work by Petronius, *The Satyricon.* Petronius chronicled the picaresque adventures of some rather unsavory characters in imperial Rome. The production of Fellini's idiosyncratic version, *Satyricon* (*Fellini Satyricon*, 1969), took place almost entirely inside a studio, the famous Teatro 5 at Cinecittà, which the director considered the one place in the world where he was totally comfortable. It was a major hit in a psychedelic era that viewed Fellini's protagonists as ancestors of the hippie movement. After making the film, Fellini's fears about losing his artistic inspiration were overcome, and he only infrequently turned to literary texts for the basis of his films during the rest of his career. Even when he did so, his use of literary texts provided only general suggestions, and the films were never really adaptations in the literary sense of the word.

The discovery of psychoanalysis, the impact of Jung's ideas, and Fellini's own explorations of his dreams and fantasies (as well as his persistent illustration of them in his dream notebooks) had a profound influence upon his career. Up to the appearance of *La dolce vita,* in fact, Fellini's intellectual trajectory seems to be clear: His films begin in the shadow of neorealist portraits of life in the sleepy provinces of Italy, focus upon various forms of show-business types, and ultimately lead toward the capital city of Rome and the "sweet life" of movie stars, gossip columnists, and paparazzi scandalmongers. After that point, Fellini's cinema turns inward toward an overriding concern with memory, dreams, a meditation on the nature of cinematic artistry, and the director's fantasies. In short, Fellini's mature career has no trajectory in the same sense that we have identified a single direction in his early works. After *La dolce vita,* only the artist's creative imagination provides the limits to his activity.

Between 1969 and 1972, Fellini made three films in which he appeared himself as the main protagonist and in which the dominant theme was metacinematic, devoted to the nature of the cinema itself: *Block-notes di un regista* (*Fellini: A Director's Notebook,* 1969); *I clowns* (*The Clowns,* 1970); and *Roma* (*Fellini's Roma,* 1972). The first was originally shot for the American NBC television network and shows Fellini at work on the set of *Satyricon,* a lush, surrealistic fresco of life in pre-Christian Rome adapted freely from the classic novel by Petronius. *Satyricon,* the earlier *La dolce vita,* and *Roma* constitute a

In re-creating the sensual celebration of Trimalchio's banquet from *The Satyri-con* of Petronius, Fellini presented one of the very few scenes taken directly from the literary source in his film *Satyricon*. [*Photo:* The Museum of Modern Art / Film Stills Archive]

trilogy on the meaning of the Eternal City. In these three works devoted to the mythological dimensions of the most ancient of Italy's cities – the head of government, the site of Italy's most illustrious history, the dwelling place of the popes, and (last but not least), the location of Italy's cinematic dream factory, Cinecittà – Fellini not only explores the history of Rome in the Western imagination but also creates original and startling images of Rome himself that have endured in postwar popular culture.[27]

Following *Roma,* the director completed the last of his works to reach a wide commercial audience: *Amarcord* (1973). In this nostalgic evocation of his own adolescence in Rimini during the Fascist era, Fellini managed to produce a masterpiece of political cinema, providing a critique of Italy's past that gave the lie to those leftist critics who had always claimed Fellini had little original to say about ideological issues or was, at best, a spokesman for Italy's conservative Catholic culture. *Amarcord* returned Fellini to the favor of his producers and was not only a commercial success but also earned the director his fourth Oscar for Best Foreign Film.

In 1976, Fellini turned to a personal interpretation of the archetypal Latin lover – Giacomo Casanova – and produced a masterpiece that also proved to be a commercial failure, in spite of the Oscar set designer Danilo Donati won for his efforts. Nevertheless, in retrospect, *Il Casanova di Fellini (Fellini's Casanova)* compares favorably with Stanley Kubrick's *Barry Lyndon,* appearing almost at the same time. The film's marvelous re-creation of the world of eighteenth-century Venice inside the studios of Cinecittà yielded the most expensive film Fellini had shot to that point in his career. After its commercial failure, Fellini seemed to turn to Italy's present to cast a critical eye upon his fellow countrymen without completely abandoning the nostalgia for Italy's past that has always played such a prominent role in his works. *Prova d'orchestra (Orchestra Rehearsal,* 1979), probably the only film Fellini ever made that was at least partly inspired by political events (the murder of Aldo Moro by Red Brigade terrorists), presents Italy as an orchestra out of sync with not only the music it is playing but its conductor as well. It was honored by a special preview presentation for President Sandro Pertini in the Quirinale Palace in Rome on 19 October 1978, a recognition of the filmmaker's importance to Italian culture that has never been achieved by any other Italian film director. Although it nev-

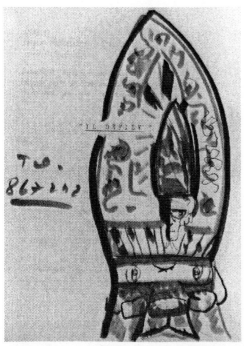

(left) A preparatory drawing by Fellini for a cardinal's hat in his ecclesiastical fashion parade in *Roma*. [*Photo:* Federico Fellini and the Lilly Library of Rare Books (Indiana University)]

(facing) Three different sketches for cardinals to be included in the ecclesiastical fashion parade in *Roma:* The figures are compared to a cuttlefish bone, a ray of light, and a pinball-machine flipper. [*Photo:* Federico Fellini and the Lilly Library of Rare Books (Indiana University)]

(below) Some of the cardinals actually represented in the film *Roma* based on preliminary sketches by Fellini. [*Photo:* The Museum of Modern Art/Film Stills Archive]

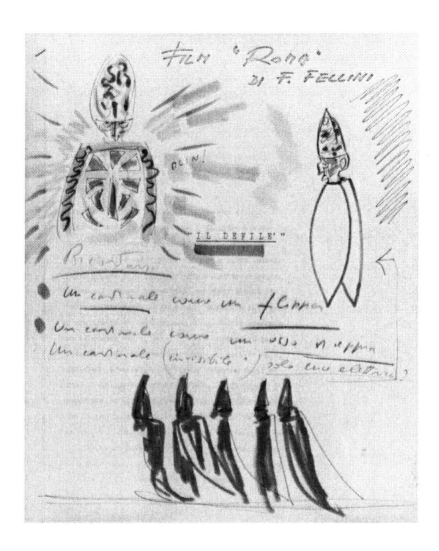

er achieved wide international distribution, the work was extremely successful within Italy due to its subject matter.

In 1979, shortly after beginning work on his next film, Fellini's beloved friend and collaborator, Nino Rota, died. Rota, whose music had become virtually synonymous with Fellini's cinematic signature, had contributed music to almost all of Fellini's previous works, as well as to such important American classics as Francis Ford Coppola's *The Godfather.*

A pensive Fellini on the set of *Il Casanova di Fellini*, a financial failure but an artistic masterpiece attacking the perennial myth of the Latin lover. [*Photo:* The Museum of Modern Art / Film Stills Archive]

On an outdoor location shooting *La città delle donne*, Fellini shows Snàporaz (Marcello Mastroianni) how to kiss the enigmatic lady on the train (Bernice Stegers), who lures the film's protagonist to the feminist convention. [*Photo:* The Museum of Modern Art/Film Stills Archive]

In 1980, Fellini released *La città delle donne* (*The City of Women*), a work that he intended to be a comic portrait of a traditional male who finds the new women's liberation movement in Italy incomprehensible. A difficult but rewarding film, *La città delle donne* was nevertheless a critical and commercial failure and, moreover, aroused the ire of a number of feminists, who saw it as the final proof of Fellini's unreconstructed male chauvinism. Germaine Greer, however, to mention only one important feminist writer, correctly saw *La città delle donne* as more than an aging director's jeremiad against change he could not understand.[28] The year 1980 also saw Fellini publishing an important statement on his life and career, *Fare un film* [Making a Film], which consisted of a rewriting of a number of statements and declarations he had written or published previously.[29] Meanwhile, in America, the musical *Nine* (based upon Fellini's *8 1/2*) was a smash hit on Broadway.

Fellini's crew builds a scale model of the ocean liner employed in *E la nave va*. [*Photo*: Studio Longardi (Roma)]

In 1982, Fellini spent several months in Hollywood, studying the possibility of shooting a film in America. After a brief time, his mother's illness recalled the director to Italy, and the possibility of an American production was forever laid to rest. In 1983, Fellini returned to Venice for the first time in many years to screen his new work, *E la nave va* (*And the Ship Sails On*) outside competition. (Dante Ferretti would win an Oscar for his set designs with this work.) He also accepted a Golden Lion for his entire career from the Venice Film Festival in 1985, thereby sealing his reconciliation with Italy's most important film festival. In 1984, Fellini accepted an offer to shoot an advertising spot for Campari, the company that produces the distinctive Italian aperitif drink.[30] He also produced another extremely interesting advertising spot for Barilla Pasta.[31] Late that year, his mother finally passed away after a long illness.

Amelia (Giulietta Masina) and Pippo (Marcello Mastroianni) – once partners in a dance routine – are presented to the television audience by the master of ceremonies (Franco Fabrizi) in *Ginger e Fred*. [*Photo*: Studio Longardi (Rome)]

In late 1985, Fellini's *Ginger e Fred* (*Ginger and Fred*) premiered at the Palais de Chaillot in Paris. Ever sensitive to new developments in popular culture, Fellini turned his attention in this film to the medium of television, comparing it unfavorably to the cinema because of its anonymous, impersonal artistic style. This film would be the last Fellini directed that starred his wife Giulietta Masina. In 1987, Fellini returned to the pinnacle of critical success with *Intervista* [Interview], a cinematic account of himself, his cinema, and his view of the process of artistic creation. Presented outside the competition at the Cannes Film Festival (where it received a tremendous standing ovation), the film was awarded first prize at the Moscow Film Festival.

The remainder of Fellini's life would mark the most difficult stage in his career. Although he was considered practically the embodiment

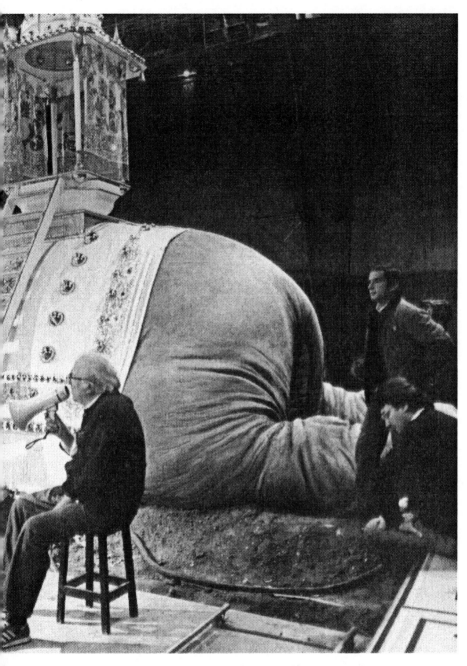

Fellini on the set of his penultimate picture, *Intervista*. [*Photo:* The Museum of Modern Art/Film Stills Archive]

of the European "art" film, his films had not done well at the box office for some time. In fact, *Amarcord* was his last smash hit. Unlike his other European colleagues, who seemed to find a transition to Hollywood an easy matter, Fellini never felt comfortable with the idea of shooting a film outside Italy or outside Cinecittà, even though, from the time of *La strada,* he could have easily done so. Limiting his possibilities to Italy by his own choice, Fellini found himself in some difficulty, since many of his old producers had either retired or were unwilling to invest funds in his various projects. Nevertheless, in 1990, he did release his final feature film, *La voce della luna (The Voice of the Moon)*, which continued the social critique of contemporary Italy he had begun with *Ginger e Fred.* Fellini's final work represents a very negative image of Italy, a country deaf to the messages from the irrational or the unconscious. The film pictures a pop culture dominated by television, rock music, and intrusive advertising. Fellini's aim is to ask his audience to consider paying more attention to their inner voices, those linked to the mysterious figure of the moon, which has always intrigued poets as a symbol of love, creativity, and poetic inspiration.

In 1991, Fellini shot three brief advertising spots for the Bank of Rome. These commercials, aired the following year, are particularly interesting, since they find their inspiration in various dreams Fellini had sketched out in his dream notebooks during his career. They also involved the interpretation of dreams in the spot itself, with Fernando Rey (who died shortly thereafter) playing the role of a psychoanalyst who attempts to persuade Paolo Villaggio (one of Italy's premier comic actors and a star of *La voce della luna*) that the content of his unsettling dreams should convince him to place his money with the Banco di Roma.[32] They were to be Fellini's final creations on film.

In 1993, Fellini journeyed for a final visit to Hollywood to receive his fifth Oscar, this time to honor his entire career. His endearing remarks to his wife Giulietta, in tears in the audience, will long be remembered as one of the most touching scenes in a ceremony that rarely avoids the kitsch or the banal. On 3 August of the same year, Fellini was incapacitated by a stroke while he was lodging in his beloved Grand Hotel in Rimini. After being treated in Rimini and then Ferrara, Fellini returned to Rome. There, a subsequent attack killed him on 31 October. His body was laid in state inside his beloved Teatro 5 at

Well before his rise to international fame as the director of *La vita è bella* (*Life Is Beautiful*), Fellini recognized the comic genius of Roberto Benigni, casting him as Ivo, the slightly deranged protagonist of his final film, *La voce della luna*. [*Photo:* The Museum of Modern Art/Film Stills Archive]

Cinecittà, where thousands of Italians from all walks of life filed by the casket against a backdrop that had been painted for *Intervista*. In Fellini's honor, Europe's largest sound stage was renamed the Teatro Federico Fellini. His funeral took place in Santa Maria degli Angeli, and he was eventually buried in Rimini. There, his tomb is marked by a statue executed by Alberto Pomodoro; its abstract shape recalls the course of the ocean liner *Rex* in *Amarcord*. Shortly thereafter (23 May 1994), Giulietta Masina passed away as well. The passage of time has underscored the fact that Federico Fellini was Italy's most original contribution to the plastic arts of the twentieth century. His brilliant career in the cinema provided a unique blend of poetic invention, narrative fantasy, and popular Italian culture that was married to the sophisticated art of an truly cosmopolitan genius.

2

La strada

The Cinema of Poetry and the Road beyond Neorealism

With the astounding international success of *Roma, città aperta* (*Open City*, 1945) by Roberto Rossellini (1906–77), war-weary Europe and America encountered what was considered to be a new cinematic aesthetic, Italian neorealism. In a very brief space of time (no more than a decade), a number of relatively inexpensive films were exported from Italy and were greeted abroad (although not always within Italy itself) with great critical acclaim. Besides the work of Rossellini (especially *Roma, città aperta* and *Paisà* [*Paisan*, 1946]), the neorealist moment in cinematic history was advanced by major works such as *Sciuscià* (*Shoeshine*, 1946), *Ladri di biciclette* (*The Bicycle Thief*, 1948), and *Umberto D.* (1951) by Vittorio De Sica (1901–74); *La terra trema* (1948) by Luchino Visconti (1906–76); *Riso amaro* (*Bitter Rice*, 1948) by Giuseppe De Santis (1917–97); *Without Pity* (*Senza pietà*, 1948) by Alberto Lattuada (1914–); and *Il cammino della speranza* (*The Path of Hope*, 1950) by Pietro Germi (1914–74). Film critics and directors of the period who praised such works believed that the Italian neorealists were moving cinema away from the Hollywood "dream factory" toward the actual streets and squares of war-torn Europe. In their view, Italian neorealism represented a victory for social realism over fiction and fantasy. Those critics and professionals who supported the production of neorealist films and a fresh view of Italian life in the cinema believed that cinema should stress social context, a sense of historical immediacy, political commitment to progressive social change, and an anti-Fascist ideology. Since the goal of such works was to provide a "true" portrait of daily life in postwar Italy, warts and all, "authentic" locations were preferred to the "artificiality" of the studio; Hollywood or Cinecittà acting styles, generic codes, and cinematic conventions were to be avoided or revised in favor of realism. Nonprofessional actors would be used, whenever possible, combined with a documentary style of cinematography that aimed at a faithful reproduction of social reality. Viewed in retrospect a half century later, Italian neorealist cinema was part of a larger revitalization of Italian culture after the disastrous defeat and fall of Mussolini's regime and the Fascist ideology that had dominated the peninsula from Il Duce's March on Rome in 1922 until 1943. Because many people who worked in the film industry had actually received their technical training and made their first works during the Fascist era, there was an understandable desire to distance Italian cinema from the Fascist regime that had, in fact, done a great deal to build up the industry and to protect it from foreign competition. It is now clear to us today, with perfect hindsight, that Italian neorealism did not really represent a radical break with the Italian cinematic traditions that had been so important from the advent of sound until the end of the war. In fact, the very desire to pursue a documentary realism that was so typical of Italian neorealism was also one of the major currents in the cinema of the Fascist period.[1]

Ideological considerations, however, made it extremely difficult to say anything positive about the Fascist period and encouraged everyone in the film industry to forget what Mussolini had actually done for Italian cinema. The industry was one of those sectors of Italian society much favored by the dictator, who built Cinecittà's magnificent studios outside Rome, along with the innovative cinema school, the Centro Sperimentale di Cinematografia, which stood nearby. Mussolini was in general more interested in a cinema of popular entertainment than one designed only to publicize the regime's propaganda (unlike his dictator-colleagues Hitler or Stalin). An especially influential and highly vocal group of Marxist critics were intent, however, on turning the understandable interest in picturing the real Italy in the cinema with a realistic slant into a programmatic prescription for all Italian cinema. Led by Guido Aristarco, the foremost Marxist film historian and the editor of the journal *Cinema Nuovo,* such individuals attempted to replace the

Catholic tone of prewar Italian culture with that of postwar Marxist ideology: They saw the cinema as a weapon in an ideological battle and would oppose any successful work that ignored what they considered to be the most pressing social or economic concerns of the postwar period or embodied a nonmaterialist view of the world. Of course, a few Italian directors (Visconti and De Santis, in particular) proclaimed themselves to be Marxists, but the often dogmatic demands for "realism" in the cinema as a political force that would agitate for radical social change in Italy came primarily from the intellectuals, not the directors or screenwriters.

It is interesting to note that the most interesting literary works of the postwar, neorealist period – usually identified as literary neorealism – represented quite the opposite of a radical naturalism. The novels that still define Italy's important literary contribution to the immediate postwar culture in this decade – Elio Vittorini's *In Sicily* (1941); Cesare Pavese's *The Moon and the Bonfires* (1951); Carlo Levi's *Christ Stopped at Eboli* (1945); or Italo Calvino's *The Path to the Nest of Spiders* (1947) – embodied an aesthetic that dealt with social reality in a symbolic or mythical fashion and employed highly subjective and often unreliable narrative voices. In short, they present an clearly antinaturalistic narrative stance quite contrary to the canons of literary realism established by the novel in the late nineteenth century in Europe or to the canons of cinematic neorealism proposed by leftist film critics at the time. In fact, Italian filmmakers and Italian novelists were trying to reach the same goal in different art forms: the creation of a new artistic language that would enable them to deal poetically with important social and political issues. Italo Calvino best expressed this desire when he wrote that neorealists in both film and literature "knew all too well that what counted was the music and not the libretto ... there were never more dogged formalists than we; and never were lyric poets as effusive as those objective reporters we were supposed to be."[2]

The film that seems best to embody most or all of the precepts for a realist cinema in the postwar period is De Sica's *Ladri di biciclette*. Environment shapes and ultimately determines a character's fate in this film. The unemployed worker, Ricci, is a classic neorealist protagonist: Almost all of his pathetic dramatic force is derived from the simple fact that without a bicycle, he will lose his hard-won job of hanging posters on city walls, and without his job, his family will be doomed to a life of deprivation in an Italy that had extensive unemployment and was still mired in the aftereffects of the disastrous war it had just lost. In short, Ricci's material circumstances determine his nature; and since he is typical of the workers of the period before the economic boom thrust Italy into the ranks of major industrial powers, De Sica's unfortunate individual who loses his bicycle could be taken as a *social type*, a figure typical of an entire class. Presumably, after a viewing of *Ladri di biciclette*, neorealist enthusiasts assumed audiences would heed the implicit ideological message that drastic social change needed to take place in Italy. After all, even such a non-Marxist critic as André Bazin claimed that the film was the "only valid Communist film made in the last decade. . . . the thesis implied is wondrously and outrageously simple: in the world where this workman lives, the poor must steal from each other in order to survive."[3]

Fortunately for the history of the cinema, the great Italian directors of the immediate postwar period paid little attention to the leftist critics and followed their own individual artistic inclinations; but they were as concerned as Fellini would eventually become about prescribing ideological goals for the cinema. Rossellini, universally regarded (Marxists included) as the father of neorealism, became concerned about the unidimensionality of film characters defined almost completely by their environment or social status. In 1954, the same year *La strada* was released in Italy and was greeted by hostile attacks from the Left, Rossellini declared: "one is drawn to new themes, interests change, and with them directions. There is no point in tarrying among the ruins of the past. We are all too often mesmerized by a particular ambience, the atmosphere of a particular time. But life changes, the war is over, what was destroyed has been rebuilt. The drama of the reconstruction had to be told."[4] In the same year, Rossellini declared that not only was he not the father of neorealism but that "everybody has his own personal realism" and that his brand of neorealism "is nothing but a moral stance that can be expressed in four words: *love of one's neighbor*."[5] In fact, beginning as early as 1949 and continuing through 1954, Rossellini moved toward a cinema that explored dimensions of the human condition unrelated to strictly social or political problems – in particular, human loneliness, alienation, and the search for meaningful emotional relationships between men and women. These themes would become dominant in a series of films he shot with and for Ingrid Bergman: *Stromboli, terra di dio* (*Stromboli, Land of God*, 1949); *Europa '51*

(The Greatest Love, 1952); *Viaggio in Italia* (*Voyage in Italy,* 1953); *Giovanna d'Arco al rogo* (*Joan of Arc at the Stake,* 1954); and *La paura* (*Fear,* 1954). It is not surprising that since Rossellini was Fellini's mentor, Fellini would share Rossellini's essentially Catholic and moral view of neorealism and that they would both be attacked by critics with a Marxist and materialist view of the world.

Another significant director to emerge in the first decade of the postwar period is Michelangelo Antonioni, whose ideology was far more to the Left than either Fellini's or Rossellini's. Nevertheless, like Rossellini, Antonioni begins to concentrate not merely upon a portrait of society from a realist perspective but, instead, upon the emotional or psychological crises of extremely complex and even neurotic protagonists. Like Rossellini, he focuses primarily upon female protagonists in a number of remarkable works: *Cronaca di un amore* (*Story of a Love Affair,* 1950); *I vinti* (*The Vanquished,* 1952); *Le amiche* (*The Girlfriends,* 1955); and *Il grido* (*The Cry,* 1957). It is interesting that both Rossellini and Antonioni achieve this shift of focus away from naturalism by concentrating upon a female protagonist, something Fellini also achieves with *La strada.* These early Antonioni films move away from strictly social or economic problems toward an analysis of individual solitude and alienation, although Antonioni was personally more willing than Rossellini to define such a condition as a product of a specific kind of sociopolitical system, one linked to capitalism. In a famous remark referring to De Sica's neorealist classic, *Ladri di biciclette,* Antonioni advocated the need to move Italian cinema away from the kind of socialist realism[6] Marxist critics were advocating toward a cinema of the individual:

> perhaps it was no longer so important, as I said before, to examine the relationship between the individual and his environment, as it was to examine the individual himself, to look inside the individual and see, after all he had been through (the war, the immediate postwar situation, all the events that were currently taking place and which were of sufficient gravity to leave their mark upon society and the individual) – out of all this, to see what remained inside the individual, to see, I won't say the transformation of our psychological and emotional attitudes, but at least the symptoms of such restlessness and such behavior which began to outline the changes and transitions that later came about in our psychology, our feelings, and perhaps even our morality.[7]

47

Antonioni himself noted that French critics of the period (the same critics who were to praise the films made by both Rossellini and Fellini in the 1950s) had defined his own move away from socially determined protagonists as "a kind of internal neorealism,"[8] a formula that could easily be applied to *La strada.*

Given this historical and ideological context of *La strada,* it is perhaps easier to understand why the film provoked such controversy. When Fellini turned from writing scripts for neorealist directors to making his own films in the 1950s, his works immediately began to turn away from realism. His first three feature films and an episode in a fourth film that appeared before *La strada* moved away from the idea of a film character as a social type. In *Luci del varietà, Lo sceicco bianco, I vitelloni,* and *Un'agenzia matrimoniale,* Fellini concentrated not upon his protagonists' social environment but, instead, upon the inevitable clash between a character's social role and his subconscious feelings, aspirations, ideals, and instincts. In particular, Fellini was most interested in the clash of dreams and the sordid reality that normally destroyed his characters' illusions.

With *La strada,* however, there is an almost complete break from the neorealist protagonist as explained and defined by his or her environment. In fact, far from representing social types, the protagonists of this work are totally atypical creatures, owing more to the world of adolescent dreams or to the personal mythical world of Fellini himself than to any attempt on the director's part to represent a simple or "realistic" reflection of the world around him. In *La strada,* Fellini has evolved toward a cinema of self-consciously poetic images and personal symbols or myths. Nevertheless, the surface appearances of the film seem to be familiar neorealist territory and even obey the textbook recipe for neorealist style: nonprofessional actors playing at least minor roles; real locations in the small, provincial towns of Italy; a large number of poor people down on their luck. The opening scenes of the film show Zampanò, a brutish circus strongman played brilliantly by Anthony Quinn, who literally buys the services of a young girl named Gelsomina from her tearful mother for the measly sum of ten thousand lire. Gelsomina's chores include keeping the gypsylike motorcycle caravan tidy, cooking, learning to perform as Zampanò's assistant in his itinerant act, and servicing him sexually whenever he wishes (in fact,

In *La strada*, after Zampanò (Anthony Quinn) buys Gelsomina (Giulietta Masina) from her mother, he feigns kindness to her family. [*Photo:* The Museum of Modern Art / Film Stills Archive]

she is raped by her purchaser). A neorealist director might well have focused upon the horrible social conditions that persuaded a mother to sell not only Gelsomina into this kind of life but another older sister (Rosa) as well, as we learn from the first several sequences of the film. Fellini, however, has something entirely different in mind, and, as Millicent Marcus points out, the fact that *La strada* "indeed meets the conditions for a thesis film on poverty and social injustice"[9] is simply irrelevant. Fellini does not condone poverty and injustice; he merely wishes to speak of something else and to do so not with the rhetoric of ideology but with the lyricism of poetry.

Perhaps his departure from neorealist practice in rejecting the idea of film character as social type is the most important divergence from

The Fool (Richard Basehart) teaches Gelsomina (Giulietta Masina) how to play
the trombone. [*Photo:* The Museum of Modern Art / Film Stills Archive]

In their typical costumes, the Fool (Richard Basehart) and Gelsomina (Giulietta Masina) clearly represent comic types associated with the Italian *commedia dell'arte*. [*Photo:* The Museum of Modern Art / Film Stills Archive]

neorealist practice; but equally important is the fact that the plot and visuals of *La strada* reject easy classification as a realistic story of social exploitation. More than a story, *La strada* is a fable about symbolic figures, and its plot structure reflects this origin in the fable or fairy tale. More than social types or dramatic characters, Gelsomina, Zampanò, and the strange acrobat they encounter named Il Matto or the Fool (played brilliantly by another foreign actor, Richard Basehart) are the opposite of social types that represent Italian reality; nor are they really traditional cinematic characters whose lives develop in significant psychological ways during the course of the film. Rather, they seem to be modern versions of stock characters from the Italian *commedia dell'arte,* an art form with origins in Roman comedy and a long history of representation that has survived from the Renaissance through the

Gelsomina (Giulietta Masina), praised by critics as the "female Charlie Chaplin," displays her unforgettable face. [*Photo:* The Museum of Modern Art/Film Stills Archive]

present-day theatrical antics of Nobel Prize winner Dario Fo. The fact that they are itinerant performers and almost gypsies naturally underlines their traditional links to this Italian comic style. Like the various types from the *commedia dell'arte,* Gelsomina, Zampanò, and the Fool are usually dressed in circuslike costumes that identify them to the spectator as stock types. Moreover, they retain their characteristic dress throughout the film, which not only marks them as comic types but also sets them clearly apart from the other, "normal" people in the film.

Fellini agreed with both Rossellini and Antonioni that Italian cinema needed to pass beyond a dogmatic, Marxist approach to social reality, dealing poetically with other equally compelling personal or emotional problems. Communication of information, especially ideologically tinted information, was never Fellini's goal. As he once stated, "I don't want to demonstrate anything: I want to show it."[10] In response to Marxist materialism, Fellini underlined a quite different inspiration in the films leading up to *La dolce vita,* Christ's command to his followers to love one's neighbor: "it seems to me that . . . yes, all my films turn upon this idea. There is an effort to show a world without love, characters full of selfishness, people exploiting one another, and, in the midst of it all, there is always – and especially in the films with Giulietta – a little creature who wants to give love and who lives for love."[11] Rather than viewing the world from the perspective of class struggle or class conflict, *La strada* embodies a profoundly Christian emphasis upon the individual and the loneliness of the human condition. Like Antonioni, who made reference to the protagonist of De Sica's *Ladri di biciclette* in defining neorealism, Fellini once declared: "Zampanò and Gelsomina are not exceptions, as people reproach me for creating. There are more Zampanòs in the world than bicycle thieves, and the story of a man who discovers his neighbor is just as important and as real as the story of a strike. What separates us [Fellini and his Marxist critics] is no doubt a materialist or spiritualist vision of the world."[12]

Fellini's interest in a cinema of poetry that would transcend the aesthetic categories of realism advocated by proponents of neorealist films is evident in a number of *La strada*'s most striking stylistic qualities: the ambiguous presentation of its three protagonists (Zampanò, Gelsomina, and the Fool); in its symbolic visual imagery; in its lyrical musical theme; and in its fundamentally fablelike plot that relies upon the Christian idea of "conversion" to draw the work to a conclusion. Let us briefly analyze these complementary aspects of the work that make it so remarkable a poetic vision of the world.

Fellini's protagonists are circus performers and stock comic types who suggest a multilayered array of symbolic possibilities that their socioeconomic status cannot exhaust. Giulietta Masina's unforgettable performance as Gelsomina owes a great deal to the expressive, clownlike features of the actress herself, who has frequently (and quite correctly) been described as a female Charlie Chaplin. Chaplin's Little Tramp, as well as the cartoon character Happy Hooligan, are clear visual antecedents to Gelsomina.[13] In speaking of the genesis of *La strada,* Fellini has said that when he began thinking about the film, he first had only "a confused feeling of the film, a suspended note that aroused in me an undefined sense of melancholy, a sense of guilt as pervasive as a shadow . . . this feeling insistently suggested the journey of two creatures who remain together because of fate . . . the characters appeared spontaneously, dragging others behind them."[14] Fellini conceived of Gelsomina as a clown, and her conception immediately brought to his mind her opposite, "a massive and dark shadow, Zampanò."[15] Fellini and his scriptwriter, Tullio Pinelli, had both independently thought about a film that would be described in Hollywood generic terms as a "road movie," a picaresque story of acrobats and circus performers or gypsies who wander through Italy in much the same way that Fellini had admired in Rossellini's neorealist classic, *Paisan*, a film portraying a picaresque journey from Sicily to the Po River Valley during World War II. Fellini also was able to incorporate memories of his childhood in the tiny village of Gambettola, where he would visit his grandmother and observe the strange characters in the countryside:

> In Gambettola, there was a little boy, the son of farmers, who used to tell us that when the ox bellowed in the stable, he would see a huge piece of red lasagna come out of the wall, a sort of very long carpet floating in the air that would cross his head under his left eye and vanish, little by little, in the sun's reflection. This little boy used to say that once he even saw two large spheres of dark silver come off the bell-tower while the clock struck two, and they passed through his head. He was a strange child, and Gelsomina had to be a bit like that.[16]

Gelsomina is immediately described by her mother as "a bit strange" (shot 9) and "not like the other girls."[17] In fact, Gelsomina is a bit dimwitted. As Fellini puts it, she is "both a little crazy and a little saintly" and is a "ruffled, funny, clumsy, and very tender clown."[18] Yet, her diminished capacities in the rational world are compensated by a special capacity for communication with nature, children, and even inanimate objects: She can sense the oncoming approach of rain (shot 60); she seems at home by the seashore; in tune with nature, in one beautifully symbolic shot (133), she walks by a solitary tree trunk and imitates with her arms the angle of its only branch, and then immediately afterward she listens enraptured to the sound of the telegraph wires that only she is capable of hearing. When she confronts Osvaldo, a radically deformed child who is kept hidden in one of the farmhouse attics she visits on her wanderings, only Gelsomina understands the nature of his suffering and loneliness. In short, Gelsomina possesses what might be called a Franciscan simplicity or a childish purity of spirit that more than makes up for her lack of normal intellectual skills, and this makes her the perfect protagonist for Fellini's poetic ruminations on spiritual poverty.

Fellini emphasizes the religious overtones of Gelsomina on several occasions. She is photographed (shot 236), during a religious procession, against a wall upon which a poster reads "Immaculate Madonna." Her function in the film is to become the means through which her brutish owner, Zampanò, comes to learn how to feel the slightest bit of emotion, the defining feature for Fellini of a human being. There are obvious Christian and specifically Catholic overtones in Gelsomina's role in the film; but it is important to emphasize that even when Fellini uses suggestive ideas or imagery from Catholic tradition, he completely deinstitutionalizes these notions from the actual Catholic Church. Gelsomina may be a clown version of the Virgin Mary in her benevolent influence upon Zampanò, but she performs this task without reference to the institution of the church. If she is a saint, she is a completely secular one. Her secular nature is underlined when she and Zampanò visit a convent (shots 518–73), where Gelsomina engages a young nun in a conversation about her vocation. The nun points out that nuns change convents every two years so that they will not become attached to "the things of this world" and "run the risk of forgetting the most important thing of all, which is God" and then remarks: "We both travel around. You follow your husband and I follow mine" (shot 539). Gelsomina rejects staying at the convent and feels her place is with her brute of a husband.

Earlier in an important and extremely famous sequence of the film, Gelsomina has another religiously charged conversation with the Fool, who relates to Gelsomina the Parable of the Pebble (shots 462–9). The Fool convinces Gelsomina that she must have some purpose because even a pebble has some meaning in the universe, even though it may be mysterious: "I don't know what purpose this pebble serves, but it must serve some purpose. Because if it is useless, than everything is useless" (shot 466). As Millicent Marcus perceptively points out, the Fool's parable moves from the concrete stone to the stars in the heavens above, and its teaching underlines the fact that the human mind, even in a person of diminished capacities like Gelsomina, "need not be earthbound or imprisoned by immediate or material things."[19]

It seems clear that Gelsomina can be interpreted only as a symbolic figure, a stock comic character or clown upon which Fellini appends his poetic themes and with whom his poetic images are associated. Like most poetic images, Gelsomina is an ambiguous figure, capable of sustaining many layers of interpretation. The same may be said for the two male protagonists, Zampanò and the Fool. Each is associated with a very different kind of character – the first is a brute, an animal, whose association with Gelsomina seems highly improbable but ultimately results in some change in his sensibility; the second is a kind of malevolent angel who delivers the message of the film to Gelsomina (that contained in his famous Parable of the Pebble) but who then concludes his sermon by declaring that "I don't need anybody" (shot 473). The two figures could not be more different: Zampanò performs what can only be described as an imbecilic strongman act, breaking a chain with his chest muscles, while the Fool is a skillful acrobat, musician, and jokester. Nevertheless, at the close of the film, Zampanò repeats the declaration of the Fool: "I don't need . . . I don't need anybody!" (shot 740). The images associated with these two male protagonists are as ambiguous and as poetic as those we link to Gelsomina: They demand explication and interpretation, but they are susceptible of no simple examination based upon content.

Nino Rota's music became internationally famous with *La strada,* and the theme song of the film sold enormous quantities of records for its time. Originally, the musical theme of the film was to have been taken from the Italian composer Archelangelo Corelli (1673–1713), and as the initial shooting script makes clear, the music eventually identified as Gelsomina's song was to be introduced by means of an offscreen radio Gelsomina would overhear while standing under the eaves of a house while it rained, as she and Zampanò waited for their motorcycle to be repaired.[20] However, in the film, Fellini and Rota decided to use original music by Rota (inspired by Corelli) and to introduce the theme song with the Fool (shot 375), who first plays it on a tiny violin that he employs in his circus act. Since the Fool convinces Gelsomina of her vocation by his Parable of the Pebble, Fellini obviously thought it was also natural to have him introduce her to what will become her musical leitmotif. After Gelsomina comes to realize that even her miserable life has a purpose, what might be properly labeled the Fool's musical theme becomes Gelsomina's, and she plays it on her trumpet until her death. At the film's conclusion, an anonymous woman hanging laundry hums the music (shots 721–35), and it is because of this that Zampanò discovers the woman he had abandoned years earlier is now dead. At the conclusion of the film, the tune can be heard on the sound track of the final powerful shot of *La strada*. In a sense, the music has now become associated with Zampanò, since perhaps (and only perhaps) he has finally learned the lesson Gelsomina's life reprepresented – that love can touch the hardest hearts, even his.

Besides the evocative music of Nino Rota, Fellini's lyrical images in *La strada* all underline its poetic narration of the film's major themes. As every great poet knows, the difficult nature of lyric poetry involves discovering concrete images or metaphors for abstract ideas or private emotions – what T. S. Eliot called the "objective correlative." Nowhere is Fellini's cinematic poetry more evident than in this kind of evocative imagery. If one of the distinguishing marks of a film auteur is a recognizable visual style, then Fellini certainly qualifies as one of the cinema's greatest auteurs on the basis of his imagery alone, and the ensemble of metaphors he employs in many of his works are all evident in *La strada*. In fact, the kinds of act typical of the circus and the variety hall are fixtures of imagery in Fellini's early cinema.[21] The very fact that Gelsomina, Zampanò, and the Fool appear normally as stock *commedia dell'arte* characters, often obscuring their identities with makeup and clown accessories, makes the expressiveness of their great performances even more remarkable. In spite of the fact that they seem to be comic types, their facial expressions and body language – particularly in the case of Giulietta Masina – display an emotional range that nonprofessional actors of the neorealist sort could rarely achieve. By using such figures in his film, Fellini can poetically suggest that people normally wear masks and often disguise their real emotions without belaboring the point.

Other Fellini images besides that of the circus and the clown that will recur in many other important films are present in *La strada*. Perhaps the most important lyrical image in the film is that suggested by the title of the film, "the road," for it is the procession. Fellini never tires of seeing humanity pass by his camera in this kind of journey that is itself something of a show. In *La strada,* one of the most moving moments takes place between two processions, linked by the presence of Gelsomina. The first and most magic of the processions occurs immediately after Gelsomina becomes disgusted with Zampanò's emotional aridity and leaves him. As Gelsomina walks into the frame in a long shot of a deserted country road, she sits by a grassy ridge as a processional theme begins offscreen (shot 220). A medium shot of her playing with insects is followed by a long shot of three musicians marching single file toward Gelsomina (shot 222). This magical appearance and its musical theme underscore poetically Fellini's conviction that beginnings happen as if by magic and that Gelsomina's road always has a possible destination. The next shot (223) shows Gelsomina plucking up her courage and following the procession, and only a few shots later (starting with an extra-long shot 227), the musicians have been transformed into a much larger religious procession entering a small town. A series of shots (228–46) bring Gelsomina into the town and introduce her to the Fool, with his angel's wings perched high above the procession in the main square of the town. By a magical and serendipitous encounter with mysteriously appearing musicians, who are transformed into a religious procession, Gelsomina, photographed against a poster reading "Immaculate Madonna," is brought to meet her "angel," whose function, as in Scripture, is to deliver to her an important message of transcendental importance. This message is the famous Parable of the Pebble that the Fool recounts to Gelsomina in one of the film's most important sequences (shots 462–9). Peter Harcourt quite rightly believes that "the whole of Fellini" can be found in this sequence and that it may be called the "characteristic Fellini miracle," where a sense of wonder is reaffirmed in the face of despair and heartache.[22]

Another image filled with symbolic resonance in *La strada* is the piazza or square, usually teeming with people in Italian towns. Fellini, however, prefers the square empty at night, preferably after a happy celebration, when his characters are forced to confront their loneliness and solitude. We see Gelsomina and Zampanò on several occasions in this type of setting where the environment reflects their interior states of mind. Perhaps the most celebrated single shot (122) of the entire film is that which contains the appearance of a phantom horse[23] Gelsomina encounters after Zampanò has betrayed her with a floozy and left her to wait for him in the city. An extreme long shot captures Gelsomina sitting dejectedly on the curb as a clopping of hooves signals the approach of a riderless horse, which appears as if by magic and without

The deserted road, on which the characters of *La strada* travel, represents one of the most expressive poetic images of the film. [*Photo:* The Museum of Modern Art / Film Stills Archive]

any rational explanation – exactly like the musicians discussed earlier. This horse first enters the film by a sound-over and then actually moves through the frame in the foreground, casting a shadow over Gelsomina, who looks up and watches it proceed down a lonely road until the shot ends by a dissolve. To describe the shot sounds banal or ridiculous, but the effect on the viewer is one of profound melancholy and loneliness. Again, Fellini succeeds in evoking a poetic and lyric image that presents a surrealistic objective correlative for an important emotion, without superfluous dialogue.

Fellini's search for a poetic cinema is best expressed in such famous sequences as that of the two processions or the single famous shot of the phantom horse, but his ability to compress poetic meaning into visual images is evident in even the most conventional of shots devoid of complex dialogue or dramatic action that are normally used by other directors merely to indicate the passage of space or time. For example, in three extreme long traveling shots (shots 579–81), each shown from the perspective of Zampanò's moving caravan and each dissolving into the next, Fellini shoots a herd of horses grazing, a small lake from a mountain road, and finally a peaceful countryside. These three shots follow the convent sequence in which Gelsomina has learned from a young nun that their vocations are similar, and the views of nature in the three shots reflect her tranquillity and her belief that her mission in life is worthwhile. In a similar sequence of five traveling shots, three extreme long shots and two long shots that also progress through dissolves (shots 634–8), Fellini shows us a series of shots of nature marked by an entirely different kind of landscape, that of winter and trees without leaves. This series of shots follows the death of the Fool at Zampanò's hands and depicts a threatening, hostile nature. The shots in both sequences are subjective shots from Gelsomina's point of view, and without a single word of dialogue, they speak volumes about her two very different states of mind.

The most poetic quality of *La strada* consists in its fablelike plot, which is constructed upon archetypal narrative elements that seem as old as time. We journey with Gelsomina and Zampanò from one seashore (where he buys her) to another (where he cries after realizing that he has lost her forever). The literal journey on "the road" of the title is, of course, less important than the imaginative trip both spectators and characters have taken along the way. It is a quest and a picaresque adventure that serves as a metaphor for self-discovery. All fables require interpretation, and *La strada* offers all sorts of possibilities – ranging from a variation of the Beauty and the Beast legend (the Beast, Zampanò, being transformed by Beauty, Gelsomina) to a Christian parable of redemption, or even a more personal account of the director's remorse over his own relationship to his wife Giulietta Masina. There is no sure answer to the question of what *La strada* means. More accurately, the film cannot easily be reduced to a single perspective. Like great poetry, this film can support equally well a number of interpretations; and perhaps part of Fellini's message is that a complicated, academic exegesis serves little purpose unless the spectator feels the emotional impact of the film's visuals.

Certainly the Christian notion of conversion and redemption (even if employed by Fellini merely as a metaphor that arises naturally out of Catholic culture) suggested by Zampanò's anguish and tears on the beach at the conclusion of the film would anger Fellini's leftist critics. When the jury of the Venice Film Festival awarded a Silver Lion to Fellini for *La strada* and ignored Luchino Visconti's *Senso,* an actual brawl developed. The Marxist Guido Aristarco rejected the film on ideological grounds alone: "We don't say, nor have we ever said, that *La strada* is a badly directed and acted film. We have declared, and do declare, that it is *wrong;* its perspective is wrong."[24]

Peter Harcourt is the critic who has perhaps best described the indescribable – the moments of epiphany in films such as *La strada* that seem to defy critical thought, yet cry out for attention because of their great emotional and lyrical power. Harcourt believes that while there is nothing in Fellini's films that can be properly called "thought," there is "nevertheless evidence of an intelligence of a totally different kind ... the presence of a mind that responds to life itself on a subliminal level, that is acutely conscious of the natural metaphors to be found in the trappings of day-to-day life and which struggles to find a structure both flexible and persuasive enough to contain them within his films."[25] The "intelligence of a totally different kind" is precisely what Fellini's cinema is all about, for it is the intelligence of the artist or the poet, not the philosopher or the ideologue. Such a poetic sensitivity is evident in all of Fellini's important films, but few of them can match *La strada*'s perennial popularity and its appeal to audiences of all ages and nationalities.

3

La dolce vita

The Art Film Spectacular

La dolce vita (1959) represents more than just a significant step in the evolution of Fellini's cinematic style. Like such films in America as *Gone with the Wind, Casablanca,* or *The Godfather, La dolce vita* transcended its meaning as a work of art and came to be regarded as a landmark pointing to important changes in Italian society as well. It received the Grand Jury Prize at the Cannes Film Festival, given by a jury that included the French mystery writer Georges Simenon[1] and the American novelist Henry Miller. Its commercial success represented the triumph of the serious art film at the box office, and although it was a relatively expensive film to produce (six hundred million lire), it grossed over 2.2 billion lire in only a few years at a time when tickets in Italy cost only between five hundred and one thousand lire.[2] However, Fellini himself did not become a wealthy man as a result, for as the price of the artistic freedom he required to reconstruct most of the film's sets inside the huge studios of Teatro 5 at Cinecittà when he might well have employed on-location shooting throughout the city of Rome, Fellini ultimately renounced the percentage of the profits his original contract specified.[3] Fellini was never much of a businessman, and the loss of a percentage of what became a colossal return would probably not have bothered him a great deal, for his main concern was the film itself. Without the stupendous sets for which Piero Gherardi quite deservedly won an Oscar, *La dolce vita* would not have been such a smashing hit.

The film's success abroad probably accounted for the popularity of the Via Veneto among tourists in Rome for at least a decade, since this particular location was identified with the locus of Rome's "sweet life" of the title. Of course, after the international notoriety of *La strada* and *Le notti di Cabiria*, Fellini's international reputation was firmly established as one of Europe's most brilliant young superstar directors who could also deliver at the box office. However, in the uproar and moralistic protest that greeted the first screenings of *La dolce vita* in Italy, the political or cultural affiliations of those who either attacked or defended Fellini changed entirely from his earlier experience with *La strada* and *Le notti di Cabiria*, two successful works from the earlier "trilogy of grace or salvation." Before *La dolce vita*, Italian Catholics and French existentialist film critics were Fellini's champions, while Italian Marxists (led by Aristarco) attacked him. With *La dolce vita*, Fellini became the target of outraged moralists from the Right as well as from the Catholic Church who regarded the work as pornographic and insulting to the best Italian traditions, whereas the Marxist Left defended Fellini for what it now regarded as a courageous dissection of bourgeois decadence and moral corruption!

Enormous social and economic changes in Italy prepared the way for the film's reception. As the film was being prepared in 1958, Italy was in the midst of what would eventually be called the "economic miracle."[4] Italy leapt from being almost an underdeveloped country into an age of rapid and unparalleled economic growth fueled by massive increases in exports of such popular products as Vespa motor scooters, Fiat automobiles, Olivetti typewriters, and (at least within Europe) extremely popular home appliances. The rapid growth in the Italian economy and the country's standard of living took place as vast numbers of Southern Italians migrated from the impoverished areas in the Italian Mezzogiorno to the industrial zones of the North as well as to other European countries, especially Switzerland and Germany. One of the immediate results of this new social mobility was an almost instantaneous drop of interest in religious sentiment in Italy. This may explain, at least in part, why so many of the Catholic clerical hierarchy reacted so violently against *La dolce vita* when it first appeared, since they regarded it as a film that not only reflected a decline of religious fervor in Italy but as a work of art that was actually instrumental in pulling the faithful away from the church. Besides being caught up in a fundamental shift in religious values in Italy, *La dolce vita* also became a battleground between the Right and the Left, much as *La strada* had become a few years earlier; but whereas the conflict over the earlier film had largely been restricted to film buffs and critics, *La dolce vita* became a cause célèbre that had an enormous impact upon Italian popular culture and was a major topic in the press of the nation for some time. Many conservative opponents called for censorship of the film, believing it was an attack upon Italian culture in general, while others even suggested that Fellini be arrested for "outrage or derision of the Catholic religion" (technically a crime listed in the Penal Code at the time).[5] Supporters of the film on the Left saw the decadent lifestyle (that is, the so-called sweet life of the title) as an accurate and damning portrait of upper-middle-class and aristocratic corruption, and while nothing could be further from Fellini's mind than a Marxist denunciation of class conflict, *La dolce vita* certainly lends itself to this kind of interpretation.

Perhaps a more specific event was also influential in this ideological debate over *La dolce vita*, for the most famous criminal case of the decade, the Montesi Case, had just come to trial in 1957. The Montesi Case began in 1953 with the discovery of the body of twenty-one-year-old Wilma Montesi on the Ostia beach. It was believed that she had been killed during an orgy on an aristocratic estate nearby. The prime suspect was the son of Italy's Foreign Minister, who had apparently confessed his guilt to Rome's Chief of Police before the affair was swept under the rug by embarrassed Christian Democratic politicians. During the coverage of the trial, lurid descriptions of drugs, parties, and sexual escapades filled the Italian press, and the trial's publicity was increased when it became apparent that some of the suspects under investigation had connections to the Italian film industry. Precisely because the accused were finally acquitted, many Italians were convinced that high-level corruption among the rich, powerful, and famous (the same ambiance pictured in *La dolce vita*) was responsible for a cover-up of epic proportions. As one of Fellini's biographers notes, memories of the Montesi Case were still fresh as Fellini began shooting *La dolce vita*, and a number of scenes in the final film seemed to recall this epic sex scandal.[6]

Other events related less to large macroeconomic shifts or ideological conflicts than to changes in mores and popular culture were also reflected in *La dolce vita,* guaranteeing its role as a symbol of the times. Rome had come to be the focus of international cinema, including Hollywood, after American studios came to Italy to take advantage of good weather, cheap labor, and capital derived from their Italian profits they were prohibited from exporting back home to California. In fact, during the period, Rome became known as "Hollywood on the Tiber," and with the production of William Wyler's *Ben-Hur* (1959), the winner of eleven Oscars, or Joseph L. Mankiewicz's *Cleopatra* (1963) – not to mention dozens of films of lesser fame – for a brief time the focus of international cinema was as much upon the Eternal City as on Los Angeles.[7] The kind of gossip column and tabloid reporting associated with the worst kind of celebrity journalist grew into a cottage industry in Rome with its center on the Via Veneto, where American and European actresses and actors came to see and to be seen. Tabloid photography became one of the most popular means of chronicling this kind of Roman movie-star personality cult, and the age gave birth to the phenomenon known as the paparazzi. Fellini's *La dolce vita* captured the spirit of this tabloid sensationalism; the name of one of the photographers in his film (Walter Paparazzo) is actually the origin of the English word "paparazzi." A number of the famous sequences from the film (the "orgy" sequence at the beach, the scene in which Anita Ekberg wades into the Trevi Fountain) actually were chronicled by such paparazzi as Pierluigi Praturlon and Tazio Secchiaroli, both of whom became Fellini's set photographers on a number of his works.[8] The world of the Via Veneto as reported by the paparazzi and the tabloids reached the heights of notoriety during the notoriously public love affair between Elizabeth Taylor and Richard Burton during the Roman filming of *Cleopatra* in 1962.

The production of *La dolce vita* was so complex and involved such an investment of resources that it can easily be termed an art film colossal or spectacular. In the first place, it was an extremely lengthy film (175 min.). Over eighty different locations were employed in it, and the cast was enormous, the number of actors and bit-part players running into the hundreds. The Italian script includes four full pages of actor credits, listing over 120 different speaking parts. Fellini's original screenplay divided the script into 104 separate scenes. Many critics have attempted to shuffle this vast kaleidoscope of characters and sets into some tidier organization, hoping to discover the film's "meaning" through such a search for structure. However, it is part of its originality that *La dolce vita* avoids traditional dramatic plotting and relies, instead, upon the power of visual images to move the spectator's attention along a vast journey through what might well be described as a modern-day version of Dante's *Divine Comedy*,[9] where Marcello Rubini (a journalist with serious literary ambitions, played brilliantly by Marcello Mastroianni) wanders through a Roman urban landscape and has a number of adventures. Thus, the overall structure of *La dolce vita*, like that of *La strada*, may be said to be a picaresque adventure – but one in which the journey has been transferred from the provincial towns and villages of Italy to the salons, cafés, and hotels of the glitterati of Italy's capital city during the height of the economic boom. Wealth, luxury, huge American cars covered with chrome, movie stars, and café-society life offer a fresco of existence that is at once luxurious and, at its core, without a soul.

A prologue introduces Marcello in a helicopter that is carrying a statue of Christ over an ancient Roman aqueduct. The journalist meets Maddalena (Anouk Aimée) at a fancy nightclub and makes love to her in a prostitute's home. Subsequently, he meets Sylvia (Anita Ekberg), a blond-bombshell American actress, takes her to visit Saint Peter's and another nightclub (one supposedly fashioned from the ancient ruins of the Baths of Caracalla). In the wee hours of dawn, Sylvia wades into the Trevi Fountain, followed by a mesmerized Marcello. Marcello then encounters an intellectual friend named Steiner (Alain Cuny) and accompanies his fiancée Emma (Yvonne Fourneaux) and the photographer Paparazzo (Walter Santesso) to the outskirts of town, where two small children claim they have seen the Madonna. In an age where image is everything and substance counts for little, the event is captured live on television before being interrupted by a driving rain. Marcello subsequently takes Emma to Steiner's home, where a group of ridiculous intellectuals chat. Marcello meets a beautifully innocent young girl named Paola (Valeria Ciangottini), who seems to be an angel from an Umbrian painting. He then meets his father (Annibale Ninchi) on the Via Veneto and goes with Paparazzo to another nightclub, the Cha-Cha-Cha Club, where they meet Fanny (Magali Nöel). His father seems to have a slight heart attack after Fanny takes him to her apartment, where she has obviously been engaged by Marcello to make love to his father. Marcello then joins with a large group of rich and/or beautiful partygoers who drive outside Rome to Bassano di Sutri, where a collection of Roman aristrocrats have a world-weary revel at an ancient castle. Shortly thereafter, Marcello learns that Steiner has committed suicide after killing his two children. He then presides over what passed for an "orgy" in 1959 at Fregene, which includes a mild striptease that seemed extremely risqué at the time. As dawn breaks, the group discovers a monster fish on the beach, while Marcello tries but fails to communicate with Paola nearby. The film concludes with a close-up of Paola's smiling face.

La strada had abandoned a quest for social realism and the notion of a socially determined film character for a fablelike fairy tale of Beauty and the Beast based upon a secular notion of Christian conversion and grace. *La dolce vita* abandons the traditional notion of dramatic development for a dizzying ride through the present seen through the eyes of a director who examines a world without grace – a decadent, even corrupt world without God. If Fellini's trilogy of grace or salvation, the high point of which was certainly *La strada,* presupposed the possibility of some transcendence, some escape from the bounds of reality and quotidian existence, *La dolce vita* chronicles what amounts to a major shift in Fellini's personal view of the world, for it underlines just how nearly impossible such transcendence can be to achieve, how difficult it is to receive the kind of grace that characters such as Gelsomina or Cabiria in Fellini's earlier films effortlessly enjoyed.

It was Marxist poet, critic, and director, Pier Paolo Pasolini, who saw beneath Fellini's chronicles of social decadence to note that even while *La dolce vita* embodied what he called a "non-dialectical relationship between sin and innocence," the film nevertheless represented "the highest and most absolute product of Catholicism" of the recent past because Fellini's characters are "so full of the joy of being."[10] In fact, the paradoxical aspect of the world of *La dolce vita* is that Fellini presents his fantasy world *without* rigorous moralistic judgments. His Roman metaphor for the contemporary world of image making, public relations, movie stardom, and the glamorous life-styles of the "rich and famous" is presented with bemused detachment and is most certainly viewed "not as a trial seen by a judge but rather by an accomplice."[11] As Fellini is ultimately a great *comic* genius, and comedy is always an art of acceptance, even when Fellini seems to denounce a condition or a character for some presumed moral failing, as he appar-

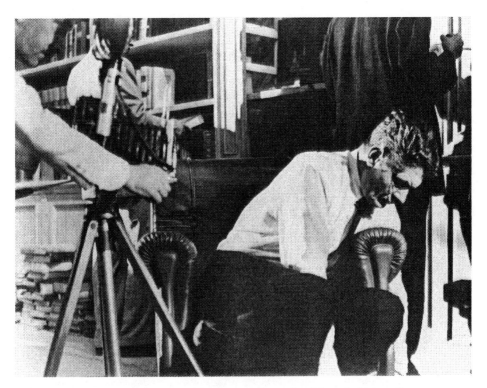

Steiner (Alain Cuny), the world-weary intellectual and friend of Marcello, commits suicide after killing his children. [*Photo:* The Museum of Modern Art / Film Stills Archive]

ently does in such works as *Il Casanova di Fellini,* before the "trial" ends, Fellini inevitably becomes a witness for the defense as well. This is exactly what occurs in his portrait of Marcello Rubini in *La dolce vita.*

What redeems the sublunary, graceless world of the Via Veneto in Fellini's film is poetry, vibrant images that paradoxically, as Pasolini perceptively argued, were so full of life that they overwhelm any sense of futility, corruption, and despair. A few years after the international success of *La dolce vita,* Fellini told a writer for *The New Yorker:* "Movies now have gone past the phase of prose narrative and are coming nearer and nearer to poetry. I am trying to free my work from certain constructions – a story with a beginning, a development, an ending. It should be more like a poem with meter and cadence."[12] In fact, what Fellini was attempting with *La dolce vita* was a modernist approach to film plot that he himself compared to Picasso's cubist revolution that transformed modern art from a representational to an abstract artistic expression: "So I said: let's invent episodes, let's not worry for now about the logic or the narrative. We have to make a statue, break it, and recompose the pieces. Or better yet, try a decomposition in the manner of Picasso. The cinema is narrative in the nineteenth-century sense: now let's try to do something different."[13] *La strada* had moved beyond a traditional notion of realistic representation of reality with a realistic protagonist. Image would henceforth be more important than storyline, the reversal of the traditional Hollywood reliance upon a well-made plot. *La dolce vita* continued Fellini's search for a new and contemporary twentieth-century means of cinematic expression, a poetic cinema on the model of Picasso's abstract decomposition of realism. It was a bold venture but one that made cinematic history.

Unlike conventional cinematic narrative, which aims at telling a story with a beginning, middle, and ending, Fellini wanted to construct a film around numerous sequences, each dominated by key images, much as one might construct a poem. Such key images would provide objective correlatives, in good modernist fashion, for a number of themes, ideas, and notions that interested the director. We have already noted in discussing *La strada* how Fellini privileges processions, parades, and an organization of plot not unlike a collection of variety-hall or circus acts. Stuart Rosenthal has noted that as a result, Fellini's cinematic narrative may be compared to the structure of music-hall shows or even acts in a circus:

> Variety shows consist of many acts, one on the heels of the next. The circus not only presents its attractions in rapid fire order, but frequently has several in progress simultaneously. The result is a dense, variegated program that moves rapidly through a number of different moods and is constantly stimulating. That last line could serve equally well as a description of any of Fellini's films. The key to the breathtaking pace of Fellini's work is its density – the packing of a wealth of detail and event into the shortest reasonable time span. The films themselves are episodic – the episode being the structural equivalent of a music-hall act. Each episode is internally cohesive, almost a short, self-contained movie. With respect to the narrative, the episodes often have only casual interconnections. They come together in a given film because they have a direct bearing upon the characters.[14]

Fellini had reportedly considered calling the film 2000 *Years after Jesus Christ* or perhaps *Babylon 2000*. Whether these apocryphal titles were ever actually considered or not, they point to the fact that Fellini wished to show in *La dolce vita* a contemporary world that has been cut adrift from traditional values and symbols, especially those of Christianity, and has been bereft of any dominant cultural center. Fellini's Rome is a world of public relations, press conferences, paparazzi, empty religious rites, meaningless intellectual debates, and unrewarding love affairs, but Fellini does not only denounce the decadence and corruption he sees before him. He is actually much more interested in the potential for rebirth that such a situation offers the artist: "I feel that decadence is indispensable to rebirth. . . . So I am happy to be living at a time when everything is capsizing. It's a marvelous time, for the very reason that a whole series of ideologies, concepts and conventions is being wrecked. . . . I don't see it as a sign of the death of civilization but, on the contrary, as a sign of life."[15]

It would be impossible to analyze all of *La dolce vita* in this chapter, but a selection of several key sequences will underline Fellini's characteristic narrative style and the way he employs one or several startling poetic images to focus our attention upon each individual episode in his picaresque narrative as Marcello wanders through Rome. The sequences that open and conclude the film are excellent examples to demonstrate Fellini's style. Both provide unforgettable visual images that incorporate a number of Fellini's themes. The opening sequence of the film is justly famous: It features a helicopter carrying a statue of Jesus (called Christ the Laborer in the script) with its outstretched arms giving an ironic benediction to the city underneath. Immediately following the opening credits, we see this statue passing over an ancient Roman aqueduct, and the imaginative shot manages to combine Rome's present (the helicopter), Rome's ancient Roman legacy (the imposing aqueduct structure), and Rome's Christian identity as the seat of the Roman Catholic Church (the statue). One of Fellini's major themes in the film is the juxtaposition of Rome's heroic past with its more prosaic present, and this opening image captures this idea without even the necessity of dialogue. After Marcello and Paparazzo (who follow the helicopter with the statue in another helicopter) dally over one of the high-rise buildings in Rome to buzz several women sunbathing and attempt, without success, to obtain their telephone numbers, we are shown the dome of Saint Peter's Cathedral, the statue's destination, and a frontal shot of the statue with the smiling face of Jesus, while church bells peal on the sound track. The shift to a second major sequence is effected with an abrupt and even shocking cut from the figure of Christ to that of a masked Siamese dancer wearing a fantastic oriental costume and entertaining a world-weary crowd of the rich in one of the many nightclubs that *La dolce vita* visits. Marcello, the gossip-column journalist now at work, busily asks the waiters serving the celebrities and decadent Roman aristocrats what the most famous had for supper: After a discussion of whether a prince had white wine or champagne with his snails, Marcello encounters a friend, a wealthy Roman woman named Maddalena. Maddalena is wearing a pair of dark sunglasses, which she removes for just an instant to reveal a black eye, obviously given to her by one of her lovers. Marcello puts on an equally dark pair of sunglasses. Of course, sunglasses in the evening in a nightclub are totally unnecessary, but Fellini employs them to show that the characters are playing roles and are avoiding the discovery of their real faces and thoughts. Like the masked Siamese dancer, they are essentially unknowable. Like a matched pair of night owls, Maddalena and Marcello go off together, their sunglasses intact. We then cut to the third sequence on the Via Veneto. That this is not the actual street but a set completely reconstructed inside the studios of Cinecittà is evident because the scene is shot on a flat street, whereas the real Via Veneto is a long, sloping and curving street. Maddalena and Marcello jump into her 1958 Cadillac convertible – which in the Roman street constructed inside the studio seems larger than a tank – and they drive off to what will eventually end in their lovemaking in a prostitute's apartment. In each segment of this relatively brief series of sequences, there is a dominant image: Christ the Laborer juxtaposed against the aqueduct; the masked Siamese dancer juxtaposed to the pair of lovers wearing sunglasses; a huge American car completely out of place in Roman traffic; and finally a leaky basement in a prostitute's apartment where Maddalena goes to make love because she implicitly needs the excitement of pretending to be a prostitute in order to receive pleasure from her tryst with Marcello. With these few sequences, presented to the spectator in only a few minutes and brilliantly edited and photographed, Fellini has unveiled the basic themes of *La dolce vita*: contemporary life defined as all façade and masquerade and set against the backdrop of the ancient and Christian past. It is a moment of cultural confusion but one that is visually extremely rich and satisfying. It is possible for the spectator to forget completely that such a world may also be that of decadent gossip columnists, promiscuous society women, jaded aristocrats, and avaricious paparazzi. We have been taken for a brief journey through four entirely different locations by a master showman, whose poetic powers cause us to suspend our judgment in wonder at his skill.

Fellini's conclusion to *La dolce vita* is no less impressive than are his opening sequences. At the break of dawn after an all-night party on the beach at Fregene on the coast near Rome, where Nadia (Nadia Gray) does a striptease (one very timid by today's standards) to celebrate her divorce, the revelers are called outside by a commotion on the beach. Some fishermen have drawn in their nets with a dead monster fish, resembling a huge manta ray with an enormous eye that seems to stare directly at the partygoers and toward the camera as well. Marcello is clearly drunk, and in the previous sequence, we have learned that he has abandoned his ambitious plans to write serious literature. Now, he has given himself over to the worst kind of society parties and gossip reporting, and his fall from grace is evident in his world-weary expression and his lackluster movements. He hears a voice calling from across an inlet, turns, and sees a young girl he met earlier at a beach restaurant – Paola, the girl he had described as looking as lovely and as innocent as an angel in an Umbrian painting. She waves at Marcello and speaks to him but her words are drowned out by the sea. One of the women at the party calls for Marcello to leave with her, but he is still drawn to Paola's innocence and freshness. She gestures to him and smiles, and her eyes follow Marcello as he disappears into the distance. The last shot of the film is not of Marcello but of Paola's enigmatic smile. We must place this series of brief shots in its proper context. Before we see it, we have been taken through a dizzying tour of Roman corruption and decadence, but Marcello's desire to change his life and to make something of his talents as a real writer, as well as Paola's appearance in the film as a symbol of purity and innocence, were elements in the narrative that held out the hope of change, of embracing what Dante had called centuries earlier *la vita nuova,* a "new life." We are once again, as in the conclusion of *La strada,* on the shores of the sea. At the end of that earlier film, Zampanò was forced to face the emptiness of his life without Gelsomina by the emotive power of the music that

The enormous set re-creating Rome's Via Veneto inside the studios of Cinecittà for *La dolce vita*. [*Photo:* The Museum of Modern Art/Film Stills Archive]

(above) A scene from the famous "orgy" sequence of *La dolce vita:* Marcello (Marcello Mastroianni) humiliates a drunken woman while the revelers dance and watch. [*Photo:* The Museum of Modern Art / Film Stills Archive]

(facing, top) The conclusion of the "orgy" sequence in *La dolce vita* with a striptease by Nadia (Nadia Gray) to celebrate her divorce. [*Photo:* The Museum of Modern Art / Film Stills Archive]

(facing, bottom) Marcello Mastroianni, Fellini, and one of his crew examine the monster fish created for the conclusion of *La dolce vita.* [*Photo:* The Museum of Modern Art / Film Stills Archive]

had become Gelsomina's theme song. His inarticulate, animallike cry and his tears embodied in cinematic terms – sound track and image but essentially no wordy dialogue – Fellini's belief that even into such a brute's life, a form of secular grace could descend. There was always hope for *la vita nuova.* Only a few years later, Fellini's perspective seems to have become gloomier. The death of the monster fish, which

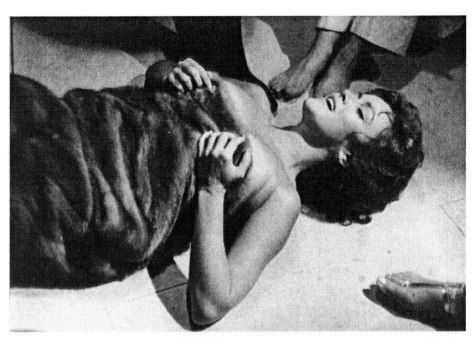

glares at both the partygoers and at us with an opaque and accusing eye, may well be Fellini's way of saying that he no longer believes in the possibility of conversion, no longer holds out the hope of grace for Marcello in the same way he had for Zampanò. Certainly, the world he has presented during *La dolce vita* is a world without God. Nevertheless, Fellini's last word is not delivered by the image of the monster fish (a traditional symbol for Christianity, once vital but now as dead as the animal itself) or the image of the jaded Marcello (a lost soul in a Dantesque *Inferno* of false values and spent illusions). *La dolce vita* ends on the close-up of Paola's beautiful smile, an image of purity and innocence that is juxtaposed (but not necessarily triumphant) over the corruption that has preceded it. Like *La strada, La dolce vita* ends on a poetic note of ambiguity. We leave the theater with an impression of utter hopelessness from the vast kaleidoscope of fallen humanity we have encountered during the film; yet the images, as Pasolini has argued, contain such a love and zest for life, embodied by the film's creator in each and every frame of the film, that we do not completely abandon all hope.

No matter how *La dolce vita* is interpreted, there is little question that the film moves along a trajectory of imagery exploiting the themes of corruption and decadence versus innocent and purity. Moreover, viewed against the backdrop of Fellini's earlier works, which were not only about these themes but also projected an essentially optimistic perspective, it is tempting to see *La dolce vita* as the work of a Catholic moralist and to react to it much as Fellini's outraged critics did when it first appeared. However, if there is anything morally objectionable about the film, it is surely not the fresco of the emptiness in contemporary life many critics believe it paints for us, which by now has become a standard critique of late-twentieth-century culture. Perhaps the most original aspect of *La dolce vita* is that its creator is absolutely not morally outraged by the world he depicts and finds it incomprehensible that others are. Fellini really never understood the harsh attacks upon his work, and he was always unable to comprehend a judgmental view of life in general. What intrigues him about the world he has created is its vivacity, its energy, the power of its imagery, and the last thing in his mind was a denunciation or a jeremiad of the world in which he was perfectly comfortable. As Fellini told Giovanni Grazzini:

I have always said that the Rome of *La dolce vita* was an internal city and that the title of the film had no moral or denigrating purpose. It simply meant to say that in spite of everything life had its profound undeniable sweetness. I quite agree with those who maintain that the author is the last to talk knowledgeably about his work. And I don't want to appear to be someone who tends, through coquetry or exhibitionism, to demystify or diminish what he has done. But I believe I never had any specific intention to denounce, criticize, scourge, or satirize. I don't stew over protests, angers, things I can't tolerate. I'm not out to accuse anyone.[16]

Fellini's unique approach to his material is evident not only in the conclusion of the film but also in the most important sequences presenting Marcello's encounter with Sylvia, the sex goddess and Swedish movie star who comes to Rome from Hollywood, accompanied by her drunken scriptwriter lover Robert (Lex Barker). Fellini certainly did not invent the fact that Italian men have long been attracted to blondes, since this has been the case as long as Italy has been a favorite spot for northern visitors. Certainly one of the most vivid memories Fellini retained from his childhood in Rimini, where the Italian men would engage in contests during the tourist season to see who could seduce the most foreigners, was the mysterious Nordic beauties who inhabited the Grand Hotel there. The kind of sexual frenzy Italian males could undergo in the presence of a beautiful woman is underscored by a famous scene in Michelangelo Antonioni's *L'avventura,* the other significant film released during the year of *La dolce vita:* In that much more sober film, Southern Italian men nearly cause a riot over their sexual attentions to a lovely woman in a small Sicilian town. It would be difficult to overestimate the impact that the physical beauty of Anita Ekberg had on Fellini or the Italians who lined up for hours to see the film when it was first released. In fact, when journalists mention *La dolce vita* to Fellini, the director has remarked:

I answer right away, as in word association tests: Anita Ekberg! Twenty-five years after the film, its title, its image are still inseparable from Anita. I saw her for the first time in a full page photograph in an American magazine: a powerful panther playing the mischievous young girl, astride the banister of a stairway. "My god" – I thought – "don't ever let me meet her!" That sense of the marvelous,

of a hypnotic stupor, of the disbelief one feels confronting exception-
al creatures like the giraffe, the elephant, the baobab tree I felt again
several years later when I saw her coming toward me in the garden
of the Hôtel de la Ville. . . . I seemed to be discovering the platon-
ic reality of things, of elements, and in a total stupor I murmured
to myself: "Ah, these are ear lobes, there are gums, this is human
skin."[17]

Fellini devotes a number of key sequences of the first half of *La dolce
vita* to Sylvia. In rapid succession, his narrative unfolds the following
events:

1. Sylvia's dramatic arrival at Ciampino Airport, where she is assailed
   by paparazzi and journalists;
2. her drive into the center of Rome in an American car, a 1958 Ford
   Fairlane convertible;
3. her press conference in her suite at the Hotel Excelsior on the Via
   Veneto (in which her hilarious answers to the press corps of Rome
   are cross-cut with a telephone conversation between Marcello,
   who is covering the conference, and his fiancée Emma, who is having a fit of jealousy over Marcello's attention to Sylvia);
4. Sylvia's climb to the dome of Saint Peter's, followed by Marcello
   joining her on the top of the church;
5. Sylvia's visit to a Roman nightclub, supposedly built into the ruins
   of the Baths of Caracalla;
6. Sylvia's drive around Rome with Marcello in a Triumph convertible;
7. the visit to the Trevi Fountain in the wee hours of the morning;
8. Sylvia's return with Marcello to the Hotel Excelsior at dawn and
   their confrontation with Robert, her husband.

The manner in which Fellini moves rapidly from one sequence about
Sylvia to another, building, as he goes, an intricate series of images
around her character, presents his mature directorial style in as forceful
a manner as possible. The portion of *La dolce vita* devoted to Sylvia
not only reveals much about Fellini's style but also underscores something that is often lost in discussions of Fellini's symbolic or poetic imagery – the comic framework within which the entire series of sequences takes place. During the shooting of his next film, *8 1/2*, Fellini
had attached a note to his camera which read: "Remember that this is

a comic film."[18] In fact, this note might well be the leitmotif for all of Fellini's works, *La dolce vita* included. It is an indispensable aspect of Fellini's perspective on the subject matter he treats that it be viewed through a comic lens. It is precisely because Fellini's works are fundamentally comic that he takes no moral stands and pronounces no jeremiads against the figures he has created: Where others see corruption and decadence in the world of *La dolce vita,* Fellini sees a kind of animalistic and vital energy that fascinates him and absolves his weak protagonists of any ultimate blame for their misfortunes.

Thus, the paradoxical nature of Sylvia's role in *La dolce vita* is that she serves both a highly symbolic function in the film, bearing the weight of a number of key ideas that inform the entire work, and she is also a shallow figure, a bubble-head actress whose interviews underscore her ignorance and her complete naïveté. No director better than Fellini has chronicled the empty rituals and the inane press conferences associated with the industry of the cinema itself, and on one level, Sylvia allows Fellini to use his own artistic medium as a metaphor for false communication, one of his favorite themes. Thus, the endless flashing of the paparazzi's cameras that occurs through the Sylvia routine, both day and night, are meant to emphasize just how little light these predatory photographers shed on anything of any real importance.

The sequence identified as Sylvia no. 1 above is a wonderful example of how Fellini skillfully creates a comic mood. As Sylvia arrives and the paparazzi explode their cameras toward the Alitalia plane that has stopped on the Ciampino runway, Sylvia starts down the ladder, her eyes hidden by a pair of dark sunglasses (as we have already seen, one of Fellini's favorite props). She descends but some of the photographers need more pictures, so she repeats her entrance, blowing kisses to the crowd of men practically in heat until they request that she remove her sunglasses. Suddenly her expression changes to a stern rebuke and she refuses. Her producer arrives with a man carrying a Neapolitan pizza, and the radio announcer declares: "The beautiful Sylvia bites into a typical and tasty Italian product. And with her vivacious coloring and her perfume, she really seems to symbolize the gaiety and the happiness of our country."[19] The sequence quickly turns to a procession of cars, including the Ford convertible carrying Sylvia, which moves up the old Appian Way into the city of Rome. Sylvia's only comment on this historic spot is the ludicrous remark to her secretary: "Oh Edna, look at

Sylvia (Anita Ekberg) arrives at Rome's airport. [*Photo:* The Museum of Modern Art / Film Stills Archive]

all the chickens!" An abrupt cut takes us into Sylvia's suite in the Hotel Excelsior in the third sequence, where the sex queen, with the assistance of an interpreter and prompter, is responding to a series of inane questions. Her conversation is actually a parody of the kinds of press conferences Marilyn Monroe was reputed to give. For example, when

asked if she sleeps in pajamas or a nightgown, her response ("I sleep in only two drops of French perfume") obviously repeats one of the remarks attributed to the American actress. Fellini cannot resist a poke at his Marxist detractors from the past, for one of the questions, delivered in a pretentious and professorial manner, asks Sylvia if Italian neorealism is dead for the modern cinema, and before she can reply, revealing what is most likely a complete lack of interest or information on Italian neorealism, her interpreter barks "Say alive," and Sylvia dutifully says "Alive," which is followed by enthusiastic applause from the press corps. Other clichés follow in rapid succession: The happiest day of Sylvia's life is defined as "it was a night, dear," and her secretary even delivers the answer before Sylvia can repeat it; when asked what she likes best, she says three things – love, love, love; finally, when asked why she works in pictures, Fellini focuses upon her ample cleavage as Sylvia wiggles her torso and replies: "Because they discovered I have a *big* talent."

This hilarious conversation and parody of celebrity interviews moves quickly to a large set that simulates a winding staircase up to the dome of Saint Peter's. This was actually the first scene filmed during the production of *La dolce vita*. Sylvia has donned a costume that represents a parody of a provincial priest – round, broad-brimmed black hat, a black dress, and a white collar. Continuing the insider jokes about Marilyn Monroe, Sylvia remarks as she climbs: "This is the right way to lose weight. I must remember to tell Marilyn." At the top of the balcony, alone with Marcello, she gazes out enraptured at Saint Peter's Square and innocently asks him where Giotto's Campanile is. Of course, it is in Florence, not Rome! Suddenly, she realizes that Marcello is a handsome man and removes his dark glasses as her hat blows off and floats down to the square.

We once again cut abruptly to one of the two most impressive sequences in the film, the dance party in a nightclub supposedly built in the ruins of the Baths of Caracalla. Marcello is now completely taken with Sylvia, and as he dances with her, he delivers a speech in Italian (incomprehensible, of course, to Sylvia, who does not speak a word of Italian) that is a delightful parody of the kind of Latin-lover pickup lines every female tourist has heard a dozen times every day on the Italian streets:

> You are everything, Sylvia . . . don't you know that you are everything, everything. . . . You are the first woman on the first day of creation. You are the mother, the sister, the lover, the friend . . . an angel, a devil, the earth, the home. . . . Yes, that's what you are. Sylvia, the home.[20]

The arrival of an American actor named Frankie Stout who knows Sylvia immediately changes the atmosphere of the party into a frenzied revel. Frankie's face – backlit carefully to emphasize his unusual features – recalls the classical satyrs found on antique Roman statues. (The English script even provides a photograph of one of them to underline the tie between the character and such Roman statues.) Sylvia and Frankie, followed by an active camera that is extremely mobile throughout the entire sequence, begin what can only be called a Bacchic celebration of erotic energy that is dampened only by Robert's drunken insults to Sylvia and Frankie after they return to the table. Racing off in tears, Sylvia is followed by Marcello who, after two brief intermediary sequences in his car, finds himself with Sylvia in the heart of Rome late at night. In one of them, Sylvia howls like an animal in answer to a barking dog, and her howls ignite a chorus of barking dogs whose enthusiasm certainly reflects that of the men in pursuit of her (Marcello in particular): Like the dogs, she seems to possess a natural energy that stands in opposition to the enervated and world-weary character of all those around her.

Seeing a tiny kitten abandoned on the street, Sylvia immediately picks it up and sends Marcello off to a bar for milk. When he returns with a saucer for the kitten, he sees an apparition: Sylvia wading in the middle of the Trevi Fountain. It is one of the most unforgettable moments in Fellini's cinema or in any films of the period. As the English script describes it, Marcello is captivated by the sight of this figure of exquisite beauty in the fountain: "He would like to enter her mood, yet he feels absurd. But her naturalness, her total abandon to sensual delight, pulls on him. He sees her as the figure of Eve, fresh and unspoiled in a decadent and sophisticated world."[21] As Sylvia lifts her hand from the water and holds it over Marcello's head as if to baptize or bless him, he leans toward her to give her a kiss, mesmerized by her innocence and beauty. At that moment, in an ironic comment on his own capacity for spiritual renewal, the Trevi Fountain ceases cascading its water supply as dawn breaks. Marcello's adventure with this water nymph ends abruptly here and even more comically at the entrance to the Hotel Excelsior, where he returns Sylvia to her celebrity world. Waiting for Marcello is Robert who, as the predatory paparazzi ready to snap the scene point out, once played Tarzan. Lex Barker (1919–73)

Marcello (Marcello Mastroianni) and Sylvia (Anita Ekberg) during their historic wade into the Trevi Fountain, a scene still remembered by countless tourists to the Eternal City. [*Photo:* The Museum of Modern Art / Film Stills Archive]

did, in fact, play Tarzan in five films between 1949 and 1953 and was always identified with that particularly successful role. At the time he appeared in *La dolce vita,* Barker had begun a European career, starring in Italian and German westerns. While his character Robert may be a drunk, he is more than a match for the effete Marcello, and he

knocks him down to the sidewalk as Marcello's paparazzi colleagues turn the event into a tabloid photograph.

The sequences tracking Sylvia's arrival in Rome to her return to the Hotel Excelsior and Marcello's disgraceful performance in the face of an outraged Tarzan represent some of Fellini's most imaginative and comic scenes. He manages to capture the shallowness and lack of cultural depth of Sylvia as well as the self-delusion of a fatuous and frivolous Marcello. These characters from the world of the cinema (Fellini's own world, it must be remembered) are projected against the backdrop of some of the most celebrated of historical signifiers that represent various highpoints of Western civilization: the Appian Way (republican Rome), the Baths of Caracalla (imperial Rome), Saint Peter's (Christian Rome), the Trevi Fountain (papal Rome). Naturally, poor Marcello and Sylvia do not quite measure up; and, in fact, it is not Fellini's intention that they should. The energy in *La dolce vita* does not reside in either the jaded Marcello or the beautiful but shallow Sylvia. The real energy of *La dolce vita* resides in the director's camera, as Fellini transforms this fresco of decadence into a vibrant portrait that intrigues the spectator without necessarily drawing him or her into that evanescent world.

Fellini accomplishes this miracle in a number of ways. In the first place, every sequence of *La dolce vita* is literally teeming with characters. Almost every one has an unusual or interesting face, a testament to the hours that Fellini spent in the preparation of each of his films, examining folder after folder of still photographs of actors and amateurs whose physical appearance struck him for some particular reason. The Fellini cast represents a cross section of humanity that could be found in no other director's work. These sometimes grotesque figures are skillfully choreographed by the director, and their movements are constantly captured by a masterful photography, alternating long tracking shots and traveling shots. Rather than employing the normal lens that most directors employed at the time for wide-screen photography – 50mm, in order to avoid distortions of the characters' background during the rapid motion of the camera in such tracking or traveling shots – Fellini instructed his director of photography, Otello Martelli, to use 75-, 100-, or 150mm lenses. Martelli objected, but as he noted years later, Fellini's intuition was a stroke of genius, for the particular visual style it invented for *La dolce vita* resulted in the highlighting of figures inside a frescolike framework with a slight distortion of their surroundings.[22] Adding to the visual appeal of each sequence were the stupendous sets designed by Piero Gherardi. As Gherardi has testified, he and Fellini would go through a ritual that was repeated constantly during the production of *La dolce vita:* First they would attempt to find an authentic location in Rome or its outskirts for a scene, but this search would always end in Fellini's rejection of "reality" for an artificially re-created location in the studios.[23] This occurred not only in the famous reconstruction of the Via Veneto but also with the Baths of Caracalla or the stairs of Saint Peter's. In the instances where Fellini employed authentic locations – the Trevi Fountain sequence, for example, or the sequences shot at the ancient castle in Bassano di Sutri – it could be argued that the real locations were already sufficiently "Fellinian" to need no touch of the master's fantasy.

I have focused upon Fellini's treatment of Sylvia in *La dolce vita* because I believe these sequences reflect most fully Fellini's powerful imagination, his comic conception of character, his narrative techniques, and his visual style. Sylvia is continuously transformed in these scenes: The sex kitten and buxom movie star thrusting her "talent" toward the press corps becomes an incredulous little girl in awe of Saint Peter's (although confusing Rome with Florence); then she is the frenzied dancer cavorting with a Roman satyr in a bacchanal worthy of the classical tradition, complete with an Italian rock 'n' roll singer imitating Elvis Presley; after howling at the moon with the dogs of the Roman countryside, she is once again metamorphosed into an innocent little schoolgirl who is trying to save a stray kitten and then, and most brilliantly, into a water nymph emerging from the miraculous waters of the Trevi Fountain. After these many metamorphoses of her personality that would require a modern Ovid to chronicle their symbolic content, Fellini brings her back to the real world she has only momentarily left – the Hotel Excelsior, her drunken Tarzan lover – and the final image we see of her is as a woman in love with a scoundrel and willing to suffer public humiliation from him to avoid losing him.

Anita Ekberg (Miss Sweden in 1951) was, as a history of Italian actresses put it, "maxfactored in Hollywood where she established herself in a series of comedies as a big, blonde, rather silly woman of the early Marilyn Monroe type."[24] Fellini selected her for the role of Sylvia in *La dolce vita* not because of her acting talents, which she certainly had not displayed previously, but for the particular personification of the Nordic beauty that Italians usually identified with Hollywood actresses. Her "talent," as Fellini has her admit in the press conference, was her bust. She was the ultimate expression of what Italians called the *maggiorata* ("sweater girl" or buxom woman) that was the rage in the cinema during the period and that produced such stars as Sophia

Loren, Sylva Koscina, Gina Lollobrigida, and Silvana Mangano. In fact, Ekberg had already waded into the Trevi Fountain before Fellini shot *La dolce vita:* She was photographed by the paparazzo Pierluigi Praturlon, who sold the images for a substantial sum of money.[25] Still, Fellini's version of the event, shot in the icy waters of a January night and not in the heat of August when Pierluigi shot the original photos, was not a simple case of art imitating life. Set within a complex series of images and visual ideas in a masterpiece, this banal, tabloid "photo opportunity" was transformed by the power of Fellini's fantasy into a symbol for feminine purity and innocence juxtaposed to a world of corruption and decadence that has quite rightly been called "the symbolic image of postwar cinema, just what the Odessa Steps sequence in *The Battleship Potemkin* [*Bronenosets Potemkin*] (1926) was to silent films."[26] The paradox of Sylvia's role in *La dolce vita* is that this blond bombshell, this ultimate symbol of sex appeal in the *maggiorata* style of the late 1950s, eventually becomes as memorable an image of innocence and purity in Fellini's world as does Paola, the little Umbrian angel whose smile concludes the film.

La dolce vita may be said to represent both a break with Fellini's early works and a stepping-stone to an entirely different kind of cinema. The films before *La dolce vita* focus upon a recognizably real world, although this recognizably real world is depicted in a poetic and lyrical manner by Fellini. As one French critic put it quite accurately, Fellini will now move from the world of the Lumière brothers to that much more fanciful universe of Méliès to create a cinema based upon the spectacular, dream, imagination, and memory.[27] With an international reputation after *La dolce vita* far surpassing any of his European and most of his Hollywood colleagues, Fellini was now ready to turn his camera's eye upon himself to examine the very nature of artistic creativity in the cinema.

4

8 ½

The Celebration of Artistic Creativity

For many audiences, critics, and film historians, *8 ½* remains the benchmark film by Fellini, the work that justifies his status as a master and continues to reward the spectator after numerous screenings. Besides a host of awards (including an Oscar for Best Foreign Film) received when it first appeared in 1963, a group of thirty European intellectuals and filmmakers in 1987 voted *8 ½* the most important European film ever made and, on the basis of this work, also named Fellini as the European cinema's most important director. The film occupies an important role in the director's complete works, not only because of its obvious autobiographical links to Fellini's life but also because it focuses upon the very nature of artistic creation in the cinema.

La dolce vita is the last film Fellini made with obvious mimetic intention: It provides a panoramic view of a society gone wild with press conferences, image makers, paparazzi, and celebrities, and in spite of its ability to create stirring images of an unforgettable character (such as the Trevi Fountain scene, which was indelibly etched into the imagination of an entire generation of moviegoers), its subject matter remains steadfastly connected to the society within which Fellini lived. After *La dolce vita*, however, Fellini turns toward the expression of a personal fantasy world that often, as in the case of *8 ½*, also deals with the representation of cinema itself in a self-reflexive fashion. This turn toward a world more directly taken from his own fantasy owes a great debt to his encounter with Jungian psychoanalysis, which Fellini described as "like the sight of unknown landscapes, like the discovery of a new way of looking at life."[1] Fellini had always had a predilection for the irrational, had always experienced a very rich dream life, and under the influence of Jungian psychoanalysis and his encounter with a Roman analyst named Ernest Bernhard, Fellini began to record his numerous dreams, filling large notebooks with colorful sketches made with felt-tip markers that would become a source of inspiration for his art.[2] Fellini preferred Jung to Freud because Jungian psychoanalysis defined the dream not as a symptom of a disease that required a cure but rather as a link to archetypal images shared by all of humanity. For a director whose major goal was to communicate his artistic expression directly to an individual in the audience, no definition of the role of dreams could have greater appeal. The most interesting aspect of Fellini's dream sketches is that they are clearly indebted to the style of early American cartoons, with a touch of De Chirico's metaphysical paintings of deserted Italian squares from the art deco period plus the caricatures of Nino Za that Fellini admired in his youth and imitated as a young man. They not only deal with the obvious subjects one might expect to find in psychoanalysis (sexuality and the role of women in Fellini's fantasy life) but also underline problems of anxiety about artistic creativity.

An excellent example of this sort of drawing may be found in a sketch Fellini made from his recollection of a dream he dated as 12 November 1961. This date coincides with the period when Fellini was most involved with the exploration of his dream life and was also in the process of preparing 8 1/2. The dream pictures a young Fellini as the cartoon figure Archie: The figure is drawn from behind the character, who sports a heart-shaped head of hair, around which the characteristic beads of sweat indicate tension and pressure. Archie/Fellini is taking an examination with four other students facing a professor. He is seated in a square that is a mixture of a De Chirico metaphysical painting of an Italian piazza, a church that recalls Santa Maria Novella in Florence, and light fixtures that remind us of a prison. Archie/Fellini is paralyzed by fear and cannot begin to answer the examination question, while his colleague Brunello Rondi has already completed the test with ease. The dream represents the fundamental blockage of artistic creativity that will characterize Guido Anselmi in 8 1/2. Fellini would often

One of Fellini's dream sketches dated 12 November 1961 and drawn during the time *8½* was being prepared. [*Photo:* Federico Fellini]

dream of such a situation when his artistic powers seemed to fail him, but what is most interesting about the sketch is that it embodies the artistic style not only of the American cartoon strip but of the metaphysical school of painting.

Among the most basic characteristics of a dream state are very little reliance upon cause and effect, few logical connections, and (in some cases, particularly Fellini's dreams) vivid colors. Under Jung's influence, Fellini began to rely more and more heavily upon the irrational quality of his own fantasy, images inspired by his dreams, a realm in which he liked to describe himself as a "guest" or a "visitor":

> Today I still need this feeling of being a guest in my invented dream world, a welcome guest in this dimension which I myself am able to program. What I need to maintain, however, is a feeling of curious surprise, a feeling of being a visitor, after all, an outsider, even when I am, at the same time, the mayor, the chief of police, and the alien registration office of this whole invented world, of this city that I have been led to by the shiny reflection in the faraway window and which I know so well in all its details that I can finally believe that I am in my own dream! After all, it's the dreamer who has made the dream. Nothing is so intrinsically true and corresponds so deeply to the psychic reality of the dreamer as the dream itself. Nothing is more honest than a dream.[3]

The immediate product of this renewed interest in dreams and Fellini's increased confidence that his own dream life could furnish the key to his art may be seen in a very interesting but not well-known episode Fellini contributed to a work entitled *Boccaccio '70*, entitled *Le tentazioni del Dottor Antonio*. This is a comic film that employs color to re-create the atmosphere of dreams and avoids a strictly logical narrative storyline, imitating the disjunctive, discontinuous dream state. The plot of the film also deals with sexuality (an important element of *8½*) and may well be Fellini's answer to the bigots who attacked *La dolce vita* on moralistic grounds. In it, a puritanical Doctor Antonio Mazzuolo (Peppino De Filippo) becomes obsessed by the prurient interest aroused in him and others by a milk-advertisement billboard that contains an enormous suggestive image of Anita Ekberg, the star of *La dolce vita*. Powerless to destroy the natural instincts aroused by staring at Ekberg's beautiful image, the comic struggle of Doctor Antonio's basic urges and puritanical morality eventually drives him mad. As one

French critic put it nicely, how could anyone but a repressed fool like Doctor Antonio refuse to drink more milk when the liquid is associated with such attractive and buxom distributors as those sported by Anita Ekberg?[4]

A number of elements in *Le tentazioni del Dottor Antonio* are reused skillfully and more effectively in *8 1/2*. Color yields to black and white, seemingly a step backward from the dream-state effect of the episodic film; but Fellini's black and white, created by one of the greatest directors of photography of the period (Gianni di Venanzo) is an expressionistic one that manages even without color to capture the essence of the irrational quality of the dream state. Fellini replaces the puritanical protagonist Doctor Antonio with the figure of a film director named Guido Anselmi who has obvious affinities to Fellini himself. Guido is played by Italy's greatest comic actor, Marcello Mastroianni, in his greatest single performance. Throughout *8 1/2*, Mastroianni wears a black Stetson hat and a black suit, similar to clothing Fellini himself wore during the period. Thus, the film established a strong biographical relationship between the director Fellini and the actor Mastroianni that has all too often been used to explain the meaning of the Fellini films in which Mastroianni appears. The plot of the film moves beyond the satirical and polemical purpose of *Le tentazioni del Dottor Antonio,* which was primarily an artistic response to the moralistic attacks on *La dolce vita.* Now, the entire narrative focuses upon the extremely complex fantasy life of a film director who is in the midst of a crisis of inspiration and creativity, not unlike one Fellini himself experienced at the beginning of work on the film. Sexuality is a major theme, but now artistic creativity and the beneficial influence of the irrational in life are also advanced as key concerns in the film. Fellini has described the gestation of *8 1/2* as a series of false starts, culminating in his writing of a letter to his producer to call off the entire project even while actors had been selected and crew members were constructing the sets. At that precise moment, one of the crew invited Fellini to share a bottle of champagne to celebrate the creation of what he predicted would become a "masterpiece." Embarrassed by his insecurity and the responsibility of putting all the men working in the studio out of work, Fellini thought of himself as a ship's captain abandoning his crew. Suddenly, the inspiration for the film's subject came to him in a flash: "And lo and behold, at that very moment, everything fell into place. I got straight to the heart of the film. I would narrate everything that had been happening to me. I would make a film telling the story of a director who no longer knows what film he wanted to make."[5]

8 1/2 owes much of its narrative structure and its emphasis on the dream state to *Le tentazioni del Dottor Antonio,* but in its elaborate structure and its wealth of episodes, scenes, and characters, the film has closer affinities with *La dolce vita.*[6] It contains approximately forty major episodes, numerous sequences, and more than fifty-three major characters (not counting the many, many minor figures, including the entire crew shooting the film that appears in the film's celebrated ending). Like *La dolce vita, 8 1/2* is almost entirely shot inside a studio on huge and imaginative set constructions. Fellini had long been accused by his critics of being a *bozzettista,* a character-sketch artist stringing along episodes with little connection. Being called a sketch artist certainly would have not insulted him, given his artistic origins in cartoons and caricature drawings, but in *8 1/2,* Fellini combines innumerable particular episodes with a marvelously strict control of the overall narrative. Everything in the work avoids the traditional seamless storyline of the classic Hollywood film. The mass of visual images Fellini creates is held together in almost a miraculous state of grace by the use of dream and fantasy sequences. The result is one of the most convincing stream-of-consciousness narratives ever created, a storyline controlled by the subjective perspective of its director protagonist that jumps quickly from the "real" world of a spa where Guido has gone to take the cure for a failing inspiration to his dreams, to waking fantasies, and to memories of his past back to his childhood, an infancy characterized by a strict Catholic upbringing and a repression of sexual desire. The entire package is presented in a comic style that brings to mind both Mozart and Shakespeare in its complexity and its refusal to reduce a work of art to a mere message with ideological content.

The film Guido seems unable to make is a science-fiction film about the launching of a rocket ship from Earth after a thermonuclear holocaust destroys civilization. A huge rocket launchpad that seems to have no purpose provides a concrete metaphor of Guido's creative impasse. During the many encounters at the spa resort Guido has with his producer, his potential actors, and his production staff, he also finds time for a tryst with his mistress Carla (Sandra Milo), a marital crisis with

Guido (Marcello Mastroianni) is relentlessly criticized by the French critic Daumier (Jean Rougeul). [*Photo:* The Museum of Modern Art/Film Stills Archive]

his estranged wife, Luisa (Anouk Aimée), and a number of embarrassing exchanges with a French intellectual named Daumier (Jean Rougeul), who mercilessly attacks Guido for his artistic confusion, his puerile symbolism, his ideological incoherence, and his lack of any intellectual structure in the film Guido has proposed to make.

In *8½*, Fellini makes no pronouncements, presents no theories about art, and avoids the heavy intellectualizing about the nature of the cinema that characterizes so much academic discussion in recent years. As he stated to an interviewer in 1963, *8½* is "extremely simple: it puts forth nothing that needs to be understood or interpreted."[7] This would seem to an extraordinarily naïve statement in view of the quantities of pages film historians and critics have devoted to the work, but what Fellini means by his claim is that experiencing *8½* requires no philosophical, aesthetic, or ideological exegesis. Fellini believes receiving the emotional impact of an artist's expression in a work of art is relatively simple. Such communication succeeds when the spectator remains open to new experiences. While *feeling* an aesthetic experience is relatively simple, given the proper conditions and the disposition of a willing spectator, *describing* or *analyzing* such a privileged moment is complex, a rational operation requiring a reliance upon words and concepts that that can never quite measure up to the emotional impact of the work of art itself. For Fellini, the cinema is primarily a visual medium whose emotive power moves through light, not words.

Fellini wants the spectator to assume the point of view of his befuddled film director, Guido Anselmi, and if this identification with a subjective perspective is successful, he is confident that *8½* will provide a most satisfying aesthetic experience. The film's narrative involves the *visualization* of the process of creativity itself, as we follow Guido's odyssey through his love affair, the crisis of his marriage, and the bewildering complexity of the work on the set of his proposed science-fiction film. Fellini is unconcerned, however, with *analyzing* the process of creativity; he is interested only in providing *images* of its process and the powerful *emotions* of its successful communication to an audience. Thus, he will show the spectator what, in his own experience, it takes to produce a work of art, but he will never provide an ideological explanation or a theoretical justification for this visualization. As he has declared on many occasions, "I don't want to demonstrate anything; I want to show it."[8] It is also important to remember that Fellini's visualization of the creative process rests upon comic foundations. The last thing Fellini desired was a pompous discourse on the nature of the aesthetic experience delivered from a pulpit or an academic lectern. During the entire process of filming *8½*, Fellini pasted a note to himself on his camera as a *pro memoria:* "Remember that this is a comic film."[9] As a corollary of his emphasis upon visualizing the moment of creativity, Fellini also provides in *8½* a devastating critique of the kind of thinking that goes into film criticism, particularly the kind of ideological criticism so common in France and Italy from the time he began making films up to the moment he began filming *8½*.

The process of creativity in *8½* paradoxically involves two different films, in effect. The film that attracts most of our attention is the science-fiction film Guido ultimately never completes. *8½* thus chronicles Guido's inability to create a work of art. However, *8½* also reveals a completed film – Fellini's film about Guido's inability to make his film. In fact, the spectator never sees any of Guido's film. Even the screen tests for the science-fiction picture (shots 600–48) are actually screen tests for *Fellini's film* about *Guido's film*. Following Guido throughout most of the narrative does provide the spectator with a thorough grounding in the many problems involved in making a film, including the personal crises and anxieties of the artist involved. Because Fellini believes the unconscious is the ultimate source of artistic creation, particularly experiences from childhood remembered and filtered through the adult sensibility, Guido's childhood experiences are crucial to his adult psyche.

The opening of *8 1/2* underscores the cinematic quality of Fellini's presentation of Guido. The first sequence is a brilliantly re-created nightmare (shots 1–18), in which we see Guido trapped in a car inside a tunnel, initially without any sound, as if in a dream. All around him are strange individuals blocked in a gigantic traffic jam inside the tunnel, some of whom will later be identified as people in his life (Carla, his mistress, for example, who Guido sees being aroused sexually by an older man in a nearby car). Employing his habitual response to anything, Guido attempts to escape by flying up into the sky in a classic flying dream fantasy until he is pulled down to earth by a man who we eventually learn is the press agent for Claudia Cardinale, one of the actresses Guido hopes to put in his film. As Guido suddenly awakens (shots 19–31), he finds himself in his hotel room in a spa where he has gone to take a cure for anxiety, depression, and artistic blockage, and where he is also planning his next film with cast, producer, and production office. We are now supposedly in the "real" world, and it is here that Guido receives a harsh judgment about his proposed film from the French critic Daumier; but the dividing line between fantasy and reality is immediately blurred (shots 32–3) when Guido goes into his bathroom. There, with the glaring lights of a studio arc lamp and the warning buzzer of a sound stage on the sound track, Fellini (Guido's creator) reminds us that Guido's world is actually not real but is part of his (that is, Fellini's) film fantasy. The irrational, the dream state, the magical – as opposed to the rational, "reality," and the mundane – constitute the territory staked out by Fellini in his presentation of how Guido attempts to create.

Almost everything about the narrative presenting Guido's work and life emphasizes the role of the irrational in artistic creativity. The costumes of the characters mix styles from different epochs (clothes from the 1930s, the era in which both Fellini's and Guido's childhood take place) and 1962, the present time. This makes it difficult to pin down a time frame. Then the film's editing works against our conventional expectations. There are very few establishing shots upon which we can confidently base our sense of space or place. Constant jumps between the "reality" of Guido's present, his waking visions, his memories of the past, and his fantasies or nightmares do not permit any facile determination of transition from one shot to another. Fellini's extremely mobile camera does not only capture Guido's subjective stream of consciousness, however. When it shifts away from this perspective, it consistently traps Guido within its limiting frame, isolating Guido and underscoring his persistent desire to escape. Meanwhile, other characters seems to move freely in and out of the frame, in contrast to Guido's entrapment.[10] The buzzing sound in the opening bathroom scene that warns us that what we are seeing is a film is repeated throughout the picture: in the hotel lobby (shot 117); in the lobby of the spa (shot 129); when Guido's wife, Luisa, leaves the screen tests (shot 630); and at various times during the showing of the screen tests (shots 603, 643–8). The unfinished sets that are supposed to represent a rocket launchpad, visited by the members of Guido's film (shots 446–73), eventually become in a single brilliant shot (shot 767) a staircase down which all the members of the cast of Guido's film, as well as the production crew of Fellini's film (not Guido's), descend in the concluding sequences of the film. An unusually large number of the film's characters retain the names of the actors who interpret them (Claudia, Agostini, Cesarino, Conocchia, Rossella, Nadine, Mario), an additional element that blurs any clear distinction between fiction and reality.[11]

Everything that is important to learn about Guido is communicated through essentially irrational or magical means, in contrast to the intellectual messages delivered periodically by Daumier, which are thoroughly discredited in the film. An important dream sequence (shots 105–16) places Guido at a cemetery, where his father criticizes him for building a funeral monument that is too small, while his mother kisses him all too passionately and becomes his wife Luisa. Guido suffers not only from guilt but from an Oedipal complex, and his relationship with women is very complex. Later, a performance by a telepath, Maurice (Ian Dallas), correctly reads the phrase Guido has in mind: ASA NISI

In one of Guido's dream sequences, the director (Marcello Mastroianni), dressed in the outfit he wore as a young boy in his boarding school, helps his father (Annibale Ninchi) descend into his tomb. [*Photo:* The Museum of Modern Art / Film Stills Archive]

MASA. A flashback (shots 226–47), one of the most important in the entire film, returns to Guido's childhood in a large farmhouse where he is cared for and bathed in a wine vat and carried off to bed. The prevailing atmosphere at this farmhouse is one of serenity, security, and well-being, where every one of Guido's needs is met immediately by a group of adoring women. There, when the lights are out, the children recite three strange words (the phrase intuited by the telepath Maurice) to make the eyes in a portrait move. The magic words are a form of Italian "pig Latin" that has transformed the Italian word *anima* (soul, spirit, conscience, even consciousness) by adding letters to the different syllables: *a + sa, ni + si, ma + sa*. No doubt, Fellini means to refer to the "anima" Jung defines in his psychoanalytic works, particularly in his

Maurice the telepath (Ian Dallas) reads the mind of Guido (Marcello Mastroianni), uncovering the mysterious phrase ASA NISI MASA. [*Photo:* The Museum of Modern Art/Film Stills Archive]

1926 essay entitled "Marriage as a Psychological Relationship." There, Jung argues that most of what men know about women is distorted and derived from their own anima projections.

An even more important flashback to Guido's childhood reveals a great deal about his views of women. During a conversation with a cardinal to whom he has been sent by his producer for advice, Guido catches a glimpse of a large peasant woman's bare leg. This triggers his childhood memory of La Saraghina (Edra Gale), an enormous prostitute who used to ply her trade on the beach near Guido's school. Guido and the other children pay Saraghina to dance for them, but the priests catch them, punishing Guido severely and drilling into his young mind the connection between woman, sexuality, shame, and guilt. As a result of this experience, Guido is condemned to divide women into two groups – virgins and whores. He marries the first kind of woman (Luisa) but takes as a mistress the second (Carla): For him, sex represents transgression, not an equal relationship with a free subject who also is an object of desire. The church, in the person of the cardinal, is the earthly institution that projects such a view upon its members by its Catholic education.

Yet another journey into Guido's subconscious reveals even more interesting information about his views on sexuality and women. After daydreaming about a meeting of his wife and mistress, in which both are supremely friendly and happy (shots 504–8), a scene that is enacted before Guido at a café, we shift abruptly to the justly famous harem sequence (shots 509–74), the ultimate fantasy for an Italian male like Guido. The setting is the same farmhouse we have seen earlier, when the young Guido was bathed in a wine vat and lovingly put to bed. Now all the women in his life – his mistress, his wife, the actresses in his films, chance acquaintances he has met (including a Danish airline stewardess) – all gather together to serve his needs, pander to his every wish, and do whatever he likes to give him a sense of superiority and well-being. They even pretend to rebel so that he can dominate them with a bullwhip in a performance that is reenacted each evening.

Visualizing Guido's fantasies serves Fellini as a visualization of the *sources* of all artistic creativity. These sources are primarily from childhood, an unsurprising statement for a creative artist. They are primarily visual images, not ideas, and they may be triggered by any free association in the present – a tune, a picture, a word, anything that reminds the artist of something buried deeply in his or her psyche. Such images are essentially undisciplined and confusing, since they enter the artist's stream of consciousness without any particular order or timing. The entire narrative of *8½* may be said to illustrate how such images filter into our lives without warning and without any predictable relationship to one another. Critical thought is required to order and to discipline such raw material, but it is critical thought of a particularly nonacademic kind. This necessary kind of discipline will only be visualized but not defined by Fellini at the conclusion of *8½*.

Definitions of what something *is not* are always easier to formulate than a clear picture of what something *is*, particularly when aesthetic judgments are involved. While Fellini may be reluctant to provide the spectator with a verbal definition of what artistic creativity is all about, he most certainly offers numerous examples of what it is not. Such

The famous flashback to La Saraghina (Edra Gale), the huge prostitute whose dance on the beach prompted the traumatic punishment of the young Guido (Marco Gemini), here pictured in his black school uniform with his other class-mates. [*Photo:* The Museum of Modern Art / Film Stills Archive]

elements in *8½* add a comic element to the narrative and undermine
Fellini's critics, who privilege logic over emotion, words over pictures.
In the process, Fellini manages to scoop his critics, placing in Guido's
film every possible critique of his (that is, Fellini's) own work. In an important opening conversation with Daumier, after Guido's doctor has

asked him during his physical examination if Guido is preparing "another film without hope" (shot 20), Daumier unloads all his critical canons upon the script he has just read:

> You see, a first reading makes plain the lack of a central idea that establishes the problematic of the film or, if you wish, of a philosophical premise . . . and therefore the film becomes (*in French*) a series (*in Italian*) of absolutely gratuitous episodes. Because of their ambiguous realism, they may even be amusing. . . . One wonders what the authors really intend. Do they want to make us think? Do they want to frighten us? Right from the start the action displays an impoverished poetic inspiration. . . . You'll have to excuse me for saying so, but this may be the most pathetic demonstration that the cinema is irremediably fifty years behind all the other arts. The subject is not even worth that of an avant-garde film, even though it has all the weaknesses of that genre. (shot 54)

After the magical appearance of Claudia Cardinale at the spring where Guido is standing in line for his daily dose of mineral water (shots 43–50), Daumier continues his attack on Guido's film off camera as Guido reads a telegram: "And the unexpected appearances of the girl at the fountain . . . what do they mean? An offer of purity, of warmth to the hero? . . . Of all the symbols that abound in your story, this is the worst – filled with am. . . . *The word "ambiguity" is interrupted by the sound of a train whistle*" (shots 64–5).

It seems as if Daumier appears every moment in the film that an important revelation is about to be received by Guido or the spectator. Just before the telepath reads Guido's mind and we are transported back to his childhood memory of the safe place where Guido was the center of attention, Daumier begins a typical intellectual's critique of another artist (F. Scott Fitzgerald) and then makes the kind of statement that Fellini particularly detests, a question about whether any idea can be clear in an age of confusion: "Fitzgerald in his first novels . . . afterward, an orgy of pragmatism, of brutal realism . . . (*off*) Finally, what does 'Left' mean? What does 'Right' mean? Are you so optimistic as to believe that in this confused and chaotic world there were people with ideas clear enough . . . to consider themselves entirely on the Right or on the Left?" (shots 171–3). After the Saraghina episode, one of the key sequences in the film explaining Guido's sexual repression, Daumier relentlessly continues his attack:

It's a character from your childhood memories. . . . It has nothing to do with a true critical consciousness. No . . . if you really want to engage in a polemic about Catholic consciousness in Italy . . . well, my friend . . . in this case, believe me, what you would need above all is a higher degree of culture, as well as, of course, inexorable logic and clarity. You'll forgive me for saying so, but your naiveté is a serious drawback . . . (off) Your little memories, bathed in nostalgia, your inoffensive and frequently sentimental evocations . . . are the expression of an accomplice. . . . The Catholic consciousness! Think of what Suetonius meant at the time of the Caesars! . . . No . . . your initial intention is to denounce . . . and you end up supporting it, just like an accomplice. (shots 392–5)

Daumier's insistence upon logic, rationality, ideology, and intellectual consistency (not to mention his pedantic and offensive personality) inspires Guido to imagine having him executed by hanging by his assistants during the viewing of the screen tests (shots 582–5).

The culmination of Daumier's critique of Guido and Fellini's rejection of Daumier's approach to artistic creativity takes place at the film's conclusion. In a frenetic press conference reminiscent of those in *La dolce vita*, Guido's producer forces him to meet reporters at the spaceship set on the beach. There, he is assaulted by dozens of silly questions ("Do you believe in God?" "Why don't you ever make a film about love?" "Is that your basic problem . . . that you cannot communicate, or is that just a pretext? . . ." [shots 700, 706, 716]). As Daumier mutters offscreen that Guido is an "incurable romantic" (shot 734), Guido crawls under the table and in his imagination commits suicide by shooting himself with a pistol provided by his trusty assistant Agostini. After the sound of the shot, on an abandoned set the announcement is made that the film has been called off. The ever-present Daumier congratulates Guido for his courageous decision to remain silent rather than to attempt to create:

You did the right thing. Believe me . . . today is a good day for you. . . . These are difficult decisions, I know. But we intellectuals – I say "we" because I consider you one – we must remain lucid right to the end. . . . Anyone who deserves to be called an artist should be asked to make this single act of faith: to educate oneself to silence. . . . Do you remember Mallarmé's praise of the white page? And Rimbaud . . . a poet, my friend, not a movie director. Do you know what his finest poetry was? His refusal to continue writing and his departure for Africa. . . . (*off*) true perfection is in nothingness. . . . What a monstrous presumption to think that others might enjoy the squalid catalogue . . . of your mistakes! And what good would it do you to string together . . . the tattered pieces of your life, your vague memories, or the faces of . . . the people that you were never able to love? (shots 738, 742–4, 749–54)

At the precise moment Daumier begins to praise the refusal to create and defines the intellectual by his lucidity of thought, Maurice, the telepath, announces to Guido, "We're ready to begin" (shot 743). From this point to the finale of the film, Guido rejects Daumier's teachings and, with Maurice's help, reestablishes his link to his art through his emotions, not his intellect. The entire film to this point has focused upon Guido's doubts, uncertainties, complexes, defects, and his inability to organize the chaos of his life. In fact, one of the working titles for the film was "la bella confusione," the beautiful confusion. Now Guido relies upon his feelings, not the intellectual justifications that underpin Daumier's arguments, and he begins by accepting his life, its confusion, and all its defects for what it is – "Myself as I am . . . not as I would like to be. And it doesn't . . . frighten me anymore" (shots 759–61).

Fellini has cleverly prepared the spectator for something magical, a proof that artistic creativity functions through the emotions rather than along the philosophical or ideological lines proposed by Daumier. Every conceivable negative attack that can be made upon *8½* has already been included in Fellini's film, advanced by Daumier or other figures. Such critiques stress Fellini's romanticism, his symbolism, his focus on childhood, his obsession with women, and so forth. All of this will now be juxtaposed to the film's most beautiful sequence, its stunning finale. Maurice's announcement that "We're ready to begin" refers now not to *Guido's film,* which has not been made and which may never be made, but to the conclusion of *Fellini's film,* which has chronicled Guido's failure to make his science-fiction film but now turns to dramatize his sudden discovery that acceptance represents the key to his psychological problems as well as the secret of artistic creativity. All the characters in Guido's film, except Daumier and Claudia (the ideal woman), parade down the stairs on the spaceship's launchpad, and they are joined by all the members of the crew shooting Fellini's film – a total of over one hundred fifty people. Many are dressed in white (Guido's parents, Carla, La Saraghina, among others), signifying that they have been purified in Guido's mind by his acceptance. It is now the world of art that redeems Guido: The film director Guido Anselmi steps into the magic circle, the circle reminding us of the circus and Fellini's perennial interest in that form of entertainment. There, after ordering all the characters in his life and in Fellini's film to join hands and walk around the ring, he himself joins the procession next to his wife. The final shot of the film is at night: Four clowns and Guido the schoolboy (now dressed in white as a purified memory from the past) march back and forth to the music. The clowns march off, leaving only Guido the schoolboy in the spotlight, which is then turned off as Guido exits and the other lights are extinguished. At that point, Guido's film has ended but not Fellini's: The music continues and the credits begin. Guido, the adult director, has returned to his childhood, the source of his artistic inspiration; Guido the schoolboy disappears, yielding pride of place to Fellini, who reasserts his presence and his ultimate control over the entire story, a story now organized in impeccable style and snatched from the only-apparent confusion that constituted Guido's life.

The conclusion of *8 1/2* is indeed a magical moment, introduced by a telepath, energized by Nino Rota's unforgettable circus music, and carried off by a director who must be considered both part magician and part con man. Paradoxically, everything Daumier has said about Guido's film (and Fellini's film, since Guido is an alter ego for Fellini throughout the work) is basically true. The entire film is filled with pointed attacks upon the kind of thinking inherent in Fellini's artistic creations, including all his intellectual deficiencies, his mental tics, and his visual obsessions. However, when the spectator concentrates upon what Fellini makes his audience *see* in *8 1/2*, especially this magical visualization of the moment of artistic creation – an essentially irrational, illogical, and ultimately inexplicable epiphany – Daumier's objections dissolve as if by magic. As the great showman he is, Fellini realizes that he can sweep away our intellectual uncertainties with a moving visual image, and this is exactly what he accomplishes throughout the many encounters with Daumier, culminating with the grand finale of *8 1/2*.

Daumier is constantly associated with the waking present in the film. He symbolizes reason, logic, and, more important, ideology and an ideological view of art as necessarily making a philosophical statement about reality rather than serving as a personal expression or a moment

The magic metaphor for artistic creation in *8 1/2* – the circus ring – just before Guido (Marcello Mastroianni) joins the characters he has created in the concluding dance of the film. [*Photo:* The Museum of Modern Art / Film Stills Archive]

of emotional communication. In other words, Daumier represents the antithesis of everything Fellini believes about art, artistic creativity, and the nature of the cinema. In *8 1/2*, Fellini's responses to Daumier's critiques are associated either with the past (the purest source of artistic inspiration) or with fantasy (nightmares, dreams, or waking fantasies).

This domain of the irrational is, for Fellini, the ultimate source of artistic inspiration and creativity. It is crucial to note that Fellini does not counter Daumier's logical arguments or ideological statements with illogic or other ideological positions. He merely juxtaposes Daumier's arguments in the present, everyday waking world of Guido Anselmi to visually stunning (and therefore artistic, but not logical) responses to Daumier's criticism.

Fellini certainly makes Daumier a comic figure who reminds us of any number of the period's intellectuals who wrote on the cinema and a good percentage of the academic establishment that writes on the cinema in ideological terms. However, it must be remembered that Guido is also a comic figure. Fellini never really argues with Daumier. In fact, the director may even agree with the rational substance of Daumier's critiques. The problem is that for Fellini, philosophy or ideology do not make up the essence of art. They represent one kind of knowledge, but the art of the cinema and art in general reflect an entirely different kind of knowledge, a different but equally respectable way of knowing. Fellini's cinema in general, and $8\frac{1}{2}$ in particular, argue that art has its own imperatives, that it communicates a very real kind of knowledge aesthetically (and therefore emotionally) rather than logically, and that this form of knowledge has its proper and rightful place in human culture. It is not so much that Fellini's images refute Daumier's arguments; rather, the visual power of Fellini's film renders Daumier's logical and pedantic objections meaningless in the face of the obvious emotion we feel upon experiencing the film's magical visuals, particularly the unforgettable finale. Pulling a rabbit out of a hat is a show-business metaphor, but there could be none more apt for the way Fellini concludes $8\frac{1}{2}$. Each time the film is screened, this conclusion never fails to sweep away Daumier's objections and move the viewer by its powerful recreation of the moment of artistic creativity. Fellini's answer to Mallarmé's blank page (and to his argument that nothingness is preferable to creativity) is a simple one – a moment of intense artistic creativity that overwhelms the viewer and thrusts Daumier's intellectual pretensions aside.

We have previously cited Fellini's declaration that his artistic intentions are not to demonstrate anything but to make us see. Fellini has Guido declare at one point in the film: "Well, in my film, everything happens . . . ok? I'm putting everything in. . . . I have really nothing to say. But I want to say it anyway."[12] What the audience sees in $8\frac{1}{2}$ represents not a verbal idea but an emotional-packed visual experience, culminating in a visualization of the very act of creativity itself. $8\frac{1}{2}$ may well be the product of a man without university credentials, a director to whom the word "intellectual" is an insult, an artist whose roots lie in popular culture and comic books rather than in philosophy and high culture; but it succeeds as a work of art in the same magical way that Mozart carries us to flights of fancy with his astonishing music or Shakespeare mystifies us with the verbal magic of his dialogue. As Maurice explains to Guido when the director asks him how he does his act, "There are some tricks, but there's also something true about it. I don't know how it happens, but it happens" (shot 219). Fellini's masterpiece aims to visualize a similar kind of aesthetic experience, one that can be seen and embodied on the screen but not easily explained by rational discourse.

5

Amarcord

Nostalgia and Politics

It is has long been a critical commonplace that Fellini has no interest in broader social questions or politics. Certainly, he has often expressed a distaste for ideology (which, as we have seen, he defines as a willful lie designed to befuddle common people): "Especially as regards passion for politics, I am more Eskimo than Roman. . . . I am not a political person, have never been one. Politics and sports leave me completely cold, indifferent."[1] Moreover, Fellini has frequently proclaimed his belief that he would have been best served to have lived as an artist during the great periods of papal patronage, when he could have found support for his art without regard to ideological considerations: "I believe a person with an artistic bent is naturally conservative and needs order around him. . . . I need order because I am a transgressor . . . to carry out my transgressions I need very strict order, with many taboos, obstacles at every step, moralizing, processions, alpine choruses filing along."[2] His early interest in the exploration of a private fantasy world of his own making, such as we have analyzed in *La strada*, obliged Fellini to move beyond the typical neorealist attention to critical social issues that was the favored thematic content of the films widely praised by the more ideologically oriented film critics of the late 1940s and early 1950s. Since Fellini's early works did not easily fit into this kind of programmatic realism with a social purpose, it became easy to pigeonhole Fellini's films as extravagant fantasies, baroque metaphors, or self-indulgent autobiographical recollections with little or no relevance to the current events of the times.

However, the fact that Fellini has never enjoyed the national pastimes of Italy – soccer and arguing about political ideology – should not be confused with a complete disinterest in questions of broad social concern. On the contrary, even the early films that Fellini produced in the 1950s and that were criticized by his ideological opponents for their "betrayal" of neorealism are today screened for their brilliant evocation of what provincial life during that period was like in Italy. A case in point would be *I vitelloni,* which continues today to be one of Fellini's most popular works in Italy precisely because it has revealed, after almost five decades, its authenticity as a wonderfully accurate portrait of daily life in the country's small towns just before the impact of the "economic miracle" and the transition of the peninsula to a modern, industrial nation. Moreover, other important films of his career, from *La dolce vita* (an anticipation in 1959 of the media-oriented consumer society that only now dominates Italian life) to *Ginger e Fred* or *La voce della luna* (both devastatingly accurate portraits of the negative effects of television and advertising in Italy) could be cited as not only faithful representations of Italian "reality" but even prophetically accurate ones that pinpointed problems in Italian society long before other less perceptive artists or social critics had begun to grapple with them.

This kind of sensitivity to the culture of Italy that has always characterized Fellini's cinema is exactly the quality that has moved another Italian filmmaker with far more overt ideological pretensions, Lina Wertmüller, to remark: "Federico has given us the most significant traces and graffiti of our history in the last twenty years. He declares he is not concerned with politics and is not interested in fixed themes or ideological lay-outs, but he is, in the final analysis, the most political and sociological, I believe, of our authors."[3] Fellini has also been quite caustic in his comments about the so-called political film in Italy – that is, a work of art whose primary function is to make a political, not an artistic or aesthetic, statement. As he has declared,

> Good intentions and honest feelings, and a passionate belief in one's own ideals, may make excellent politics or influential social work (things which may be much more useful than the cinema), but they do not necessarily and indisputably make good films. And there is really nothing uglier or drearier – just because it is ineffectual and pointless – than a bad political film.[4]

Because Fellini is primarily an artist and not an ideologue, it is not surprising that the few basic beliefs he holds in this regard are rooted ultimately in his aesthetics. As we have seen from our discussion of *8 1/2*, Fellini locates the focal point of creativity in the individual and his fantasy life. Consequently, anything that deforms, obstructs, represses, or distorts this creativity or the growth of a free consciousness within the individuals making up society is to be opposed:

> I believe – please note, I am only supposing – that what I care about most is the freedom of man, the liberation of the individual man from the network of moral and social convention in which he believes, or rather in which he thinks he believes, and which encloses him and limits him and makes him seem narrower, smaller, sometimes even worse than he really is. If you really want me to turn teacher, then condense it with these words: be what you are, that is, discover yourself, in order to love life.[5]

This belief in the dignity and even the nobility of the individual human being derives in Fellini not from some clearly formulated political doctrine but, rather, from an instinctual aversion to all forms of autocratic control.

Fellini's distaste for authoritarian institutions or ideas can be traced back to his childhood, two decades roughly contemporary with the life of the regime itself (1922–43). During Fellini's formative years, the Fascist government attempted, actually with a great deal of success and popular support, to regiment almost every aspect of Italian economic, political, and cultural life. Even after the fall of the Fascist regime and the establishment of a democratic republic in the wake of the Allied liberation of Italy, the most dominant forces contending for control of Italy represented anything but liberal democratic political philosophies. On the conservative Right, political institutions were dominated by the Christian Democratic party (DC), which was far too closely aligned with an extremely conservative and even reactionary pre–Vatican II church to suit Fellini's tastes. It must also be said, however, that the Christian Democrats made two fundamental decisions that would guarantee Italy's future as a free and democratic nation: The party sponsored Italy's membership in NATO, protecting the country from the very real threat of external subversions and internal upheaval; and it helped lead other European nations toward the creation of a Common Market, a decision that ensured the existence of a free-market economy in a country that had always been controlled by political regimes hostile to any kind of economic freedom. On the Left, the opposition was led by an Italian Communist Party (PCI) that had been created precisely to oppose social-democratic tendencies in the socialist movement. In the two decades after Mussolini's fall, it continued to retain its Stalinist, nondemocratic character within its central committee, while at the same time, it quite successfully convinced gullible foreign observers of the Italian scene that the party was like every other European democratic institution. In many respects, the PCI was as conservative in social matters as the DC, but it carried out a very successful campaign, as a result of puffing up its record during the Resistance, to bring Italian intellectuals into its fold. One of the party's founders, Antonio Gramsci (1891–1937) had advocated a policy of obtaining intellectual hegemony in Italian society before gaining political power. Although urging the primacy of cultural over economic forces represents the exact opposite of classical Marxist theory, this theory of hegemony was highly successful as a practical policy. Italian intellectual life was thoroughly dominated by the Marxist Left much as the non-Marxist Right controlled the church and the state.

All of Fellini's films, as the director noted in a letter about *Amarcord* to the Italian critic Gian Luigi Rondi, "have the tendency to demolish preconceived ideas, rhetoric, diagrams, taboos, the abhorrent forms of a certain type of upbringing."[6] Because of his contrarian spirit, Fellini was uncomfortable as a young man in Fascist Italy:

> Commitment, I feel, prevents a man from development. My 'antifascism' is of a biological kind. I could never forget the isolation in which Italy was enclosed for twenty years. Today I feel a profound hatred – and I am actually very vulnerable on this point – for all ideas that can be translated into formulas. I am committed to noncommitment.[7]

Because of this aversion to politics, it is not surprising that during the immediate postwar period, when he first began writing scripts and directing his early films, Fellini ran afoul of critics on both sides of the political spectrum, especially those following the PCI's cultural directives that advocated only "progressive" films embodying an aesthetic bordering on socialist realism. The postwar period in Italy was thus marked, in many respects, by pressures toward social and cultural conformity that recalled the more obligatory compromises enforced upon intellectuals and artists during the Fascist period. Fellini's childhood and adolescence unfolded during a dictatorship. More than most of his contemporaries, Fellini sensed the continuities between those dark years (*il ventennio nero* or the "dark twenty years," as Italians call it) and the postwar period. He believed that Fascism arose in Italy because of a particular Italian character defect.

Fascism represents the central historical event of the twentieth century in Italy, and arguments about its origins, its policies, its responsibilities, and its legacies continue unabated to the present day. Numerous learned books advance a variety of theories for Italian Fascism (which, first of all, would do well to distinguish the Latin variety from the German brand). As A. J. Gregor and Renzo De Felice had pointed out in surveys of such explanations, a number of the explanatory theories first advanced even before the fall of the regime spoke of moral crisis, of the intrusion of the masses into history, the Stalinist theory that Fascism was a tool of the capitalist class to suppress the class struggle, or Freudian and neo-Freudian theories of social psychology that saw individual Fascists produced by sexual deviance stemming from childhood.[8] Popular images of Fascism in the postwar Italian cinema tended to follow either the Marxist line or the neo-Freudian line. In the hands of a director of genius, such as Bernardo Bertolucci, films reflecting these theories could transcend the realm of propaganda and create original images of Fascism with aesthetic appeal to the most apolitical film spectator. Thus, Bertolucci's *The Conformist* (*Il conformista*, 1970), explains the protagonist's adherence to the Fascist Party through sexual theories indebted to Wilhelm Reich and sets this portrait within one of the most visually stunning films of the period. His later epic – what might well be called a Marxist *Gone with the Wind*, set in Emilia–Romagna and entitled *1900* (*Novecento*, 1976) to underline its attempt to explain the entire sweep of twentieth-century Italian history – combines both Marxist and neo-Freudian views of the development of agrarian Fascism in the province that produced both Fellini and Bertolucci.

Although Fellini's views on Italian history are far less dogmatic than Bertolucci's, they embody a consistency of thought with links to his first works, and his thinking on the vexing historical problem of Italian Fascism represents anything but a naïve perspective. *Amarcord* (1973) pictures the life of a provincial town very similar to Fellini's Rimini during the 1930s. Though made some two decades after *I vitelloni, Amarcord* must be placed chronologically before *I vitelloni* as a companion piece, since the young boys of the second film during the Fascist dictatorship grow up to become the adult slackers in the first film. Numerous elements in both films link them together. The town idiot, Giudizio, appears in both films without aging. The events in *I vitelloni* that mark off the tourist season in the Adriatic resort town from the rest of the boring, touristless year – the Carnival, the election of Miss Siren, the arrival and departure of the tourists, the passing of the seasons – are in *Amarcord* either repeated (as with the tourists and the seasons) or modified by giving communal events a political twist – the passage of the *Rex*, the regime's stupendous ocean liner; the arrival of the Fascist official on 21 April to celebrate the mythical foundation of ancient Rome. Pataca, the Fascist gigolo who picks up Nordic tourists offering him "posterior intimacy" during the tourist season, seems to be an earlier and even more immature version of Fausto, the archetypal *vitellone* who cheats on his young wife on every occasion he can manage. Perhaps most disturbing, however, is that in *Amarcord*, there is no equivalent of Moraldo, the only real positive character in *I vitelloni*, who not only senses that the provincial life the *vitelloni* lead is empty and meaningless but who also leaves town and heads for Rome to look for something new. With his departure, Moraldo becomes the prototype of Marcello, the provincial who is the writer-journalist in *La dolce vita*, whom Fellini develops from a script entitled *Moraldo in città* that he wrote but never filmed.[9] In *Amarcord*, however, an entire generation of Italians, and not just a few slackers, is enshrouded in a fog of ignorance that is vividly portrayed in one of the film's most memorable sequences. In the lives of both the postwar *vitelloni* and the prewar Amarcordians, the myth of the cinema plays a vital role in shaping their behavior and their aspirations.

Fellini's portrait of the provinces during the Fascist period avoids the facile juxtaposition of "good" (i.e., anti-Fascists) and "bad" (i.e., Fascists) that characterizes most Italian political films on the subject. Rather than the jack-booted army veterans who attack the peasantry and workers during strikes, or the wealthy farmers of Bertolucci's *1900* who hire them, Fellini's Fascism is populated by a number of comic figures, some of whom are clearly related to the clown figures of his earlier films. Much, but not all, of the film focuses upon a typical family of the period that may also have autobiographical overtones: Aurelio (Armando Brancia), an anti-Fascist worker who has become a foreman and a relatively wealthy man; his wife Miranda (Pupella Maggio), a somewhat hysterical and stereotypical Italian mother who dotes on her son and worthless brother; Lallo, nicknamed Il Pataca (Nando Orfei), the gigolo who parades in his Fascist uniform but is interested only in picking up Nordic tourists; and Titta (Bruno Zanin), a figure often identified with Fellini himself but actually based on Fellini's best friend during his adolescence.[10] The family also includes a maid, another son, a crazy Uncle Teo in an asylum (Ciccio Ingrassia), and Titta's grandfather (Peppino Ianigo) whose life continues to be dominated by his sexual fantasies. Related to this cast of comic figures, indebted to Fellini's familiarity with the world of cartoon strips, is a group of grotesque individuals in Titta's school. Both Titta's classmates and his teachers are cut from the same cartoon cloth. They are clearly caricatures and gross caricatures at that, with no effort whatsoever made to create believable or realistic portraits of this provincial world. Even the figures in the town who are obviously linked directly to the regime – the local Fascist *gerarca* and the Fascist *federale* who visits the populace on 21 April to celebrate their "Roman" origins – are clownish figures. They are joined by a nymphomaniac named Volpina; the village idiot Giudizio; the village beauty Gradisca, the object of desire of every male in the town, especially Titta; a priest named Don Balosa, who seems more concerned over the masturbation of the young boys who dream of Gradisca than with real sins; the owner of the local Cinema Fulgor (the theater for which the young Federico Fellini designed lobby cards), who calls himself "Ronald Colman" in homage to the American cinema that is the town's source of shallow dreams; a blind accordionist; and a talkative lawyer who often addresses the camera to provide the viewer with explanations.

This enormous cast of truly amusing characters interacts together on a number of occasions: During the first important sequence of the film, when the town's populace burns a witch in effigy to celebrate the coming of spring on Saint Joseph's Day (19 March); when everyone assembles in Fascist uniform to greet the *federale* to celebrate the "Roman" aspect of the Fascist state; and when the entire town sails out to sea to

Outside the Cinema Fulgor in Amarcord, Gradisca (Magali Nöel), "Ronald Colman" (Mario Liberati), and a number of the townspeople of *Amarcord*

gather before the shrine to Hollywood mythology in the Italian provinces.
[*Photo:* The Museum of Modern Art/Film Stills Archive]

The passage of the ocean liner *Rex*, symbol of the Fascist regime in *Amarcord*.
[*Photo:* The Museum of Modern Art / Film Stills Archive]

witness the passage of the *Rex,* the ocean liner that the Fascist regime actually constructed and that conquered speed records for transatlantic crossings between Italy and America during its heyday. Fellini employs the juxtaposition between the glimpses we are permitted to see of the private lives of these stock comic characters and their public, group activities to make an important comment on the nature of Fascism within the Italian provinces. As Fellini notes, living in a repressed state such as Fascism promoted during his adolescence, "each person develops not individual characteristics but only pathological defects"; examined individually, these comic characters seem to exhibit only

> manias, innocuous tics: and yet, it is enough for the characters to gather together for an occasion like this [the *federale*'s visit], and there, from apparently harmless eccentricities, their manias take on a completely different meaning. The gathering of April 21st, just like the passing of the *Rex,* the burning of the great bonfire at the beginning, and so on, are always occasions of total stupidity. The pretext of being together is always a leveling process. . . . It is only ritual that keeps them all together. Since no character has a real sense of individual responsibility, or has only petty dreams, no one has the strength not to take part in the ritual, to remain at home outside of it.[11]

Beginning with this collection of grotesque individuals, Fellini builds upon their tics and eccentricities to paint a collective portrait of Italian Fascism:

> The province of Amarcord is one in which we are all recognizable, the director first of all, in the ignorance which confounded us. A great ignorance and a great confusion. Not that I wish to minimize the economic and social causes of Fascism. I only wish to say that today what is still most interesting is the psychological, emotional manner of being a Fascist. . . . It is a sort of blockage, an arrested development during the phase of adolescence. . . . Italy, mentally, is still much the same. To say it in other terms, I have the impression that Fascism and adolescence continue to be, in a certain measure, permanent historical seasons of our lives: adolescence of our individual lives, Fascism of our national life.[12]

In his letter to Gian Luigi Rondi, Fellini defined *Amarcord* as

> The story of a place which could be in any region of Italy in the 1930s, under the control of the Church and Fascism. It is the tale of the lazy, impenetrable, enclosed existence of the Italian provinces; of the slothfulness, the small-mindedness and the rather ridiculous aspirations buried there; the fascinated contemplation of a mythical *Rex* as it sails by, inaccessible and useless; the American cinema with its false prototypes; the 21st of April, birth of Rome. Here it is, Fascism,

the dulling of intelligence, a conditioning which stifles the imagination, and any genuineness. Because the film concerns a town, is the history of a town, is the metaphor of an enclosure, it reflects above all what Fascism was, the manner of being a Fascist both psychologically and emotionally, and therefore of being ignorant, violent, exhibitionist and puerile. I consider Fascism to be a degeneration at a historical level of an individual season – that of adolescence – which corrupts and rots itself while proliferating in a monstrous fashion without the ability to evolve and become adult . . . the Fascist exists in us all. We cannot fight against it without identifying it with our ignorant, petty, and impulsive "self."[13]

If making a comic film about such a phenomenon as that outlined above is making a "political" film, then Fellini hastens to qualify this definition to Rondi:

If, by "political" one includes the possibility of working for a society of individuals who respect themselves and others, a society where everyone is free to be and to become, according to their deepest hopes, to have their own ideas, to read what they want to read, to do what they want to do whilst realizing that their own personal freedom ends where that of others begins, then, in that case, my film is political because that is what it is all about; it denounces the absence of all this by showing a world in which it does not exist.[14]

What really separates Fellini from the other directors in Italy who have treated the Fascist period in the cinema is his comic perspective and his attitude as an accomplice of the vices he is attacking. This, of course, was precisely his attitude about the decadent world he created in *La dolce vita*. Fundamentally, it has frequently been argued Fellini begins his films as a witness for the prosecution but ultimately becomes a sympathetic witness for the defense. This sense of being an accomplice, of being placed in the same court docket as the accused, makes Fellini's attempts to attack a vice in humanity in part a lukewarm operation. Furthermore, Fellini views the past in an blatantly nostalgic light. Millions of adult viewers in Italy flocked to see *Amarcord*, making of the film Fellini's last major box-office success in Italy: Gradisca, the *Rex*, and numerous scenes in the film have passed into Italian popular culture and are recognized by people who have never even seen the film. The work was received in this manner precisely because of Fellini's approach to the material. As he notes, in spite of the fact that the world depicted is ridiculous and reprehensible (in spite of its comic context), Italians also recognized that it was still a mirror of their private character and their private history. Although false values and misplaced loyalties dominated the Fascist epoch, it was, nevertheless, the only past Fellini and millions of Italians now reaching old age had ever known. Because of this, they were doomed to recall this past with a mixture of remorse and nostalgia but were unable to change it.

As Millicent Marcus has noted, there is a clear connection between the manner in which the Amarcordians view the cinema (particularly the American cinema) and the manner in which they relate to the political mythology surrounding two central events in the film, the visit of the *federale* and the passage of the *Rex*.[15] Both the cinema and politics in the provinces are linked to sexuality or, rather, repressed sexuality. Fellini has even defined the visit of the *federale* as the crucial sequence in the entire film.[16] It is a sequence devoted to a ferocious satire of the particular style of Fascist culture associated with one of the regime's most controversial leaders, Achille Starace (1889–1945), longtime leader of the National Fascist Party from 1931 to 1939 and the inventor of the Fascist "style" that so infuriated Fellini. Italians born after the war or foreigners unfamiliar with Italian culture will probably think that Fellini's satire of the Fascist "style" is based solely on his grotesque exaggeration of the regime's comic stance; but, in fact, the public meetings of the regime during Starace's tenure as head of the party – exactly the years depicted in *Amarcord* – were actually not so different than those Fellini attacks with his comic wit. For example, it was Starace (and not Mussolini) who invented the carefully choreographed mass demonstrations and public rallies where Italians, dressed in various martial uniforms, ran rather than walked or marched (to underline their youth, vitality, and discipline). Starace was fanatic in his insistence upon the use of the Roman salute (to replace the traditional bourgeois handshake) and even advocated the use of the Germanic goose step, which was defined in a face-saving manner as the "Roman" step! He frequently jumped over bayonets or horses to demonstrate his physical prowess and almost always marched at a trot rather than at a normal pacing step. Starace's Fascist "style" is reflected in the *federale*'s visit, which Fellini satirizes mercilessly as useless motion buttressed by unintentionally amusing ideological pronouncements, peppered with the kind of high rhetoric that has unfortunately frequently characterized

Italian political speeches of any persuasion and not just those delivered by Fascists. The professor of mathematics, ordinarily a buxom woman who is first shown in her classroom as a tiger and the object of her students' repressed sexual fantasies, appears transformed in her military uniform as she runs in the parade with the rest of the townspeople, declaring: "This marvelous enthusiasm makes us young but so old at the same time. . . . Young, because Fascism has rejuvenated our blood with shining ideals that are very ancient. . . ."[17] Each of the townspeople who have been sketched out in comic caricatures before the *federale*'s visit is suddenly transformed by donning a uniform and joining others in what Fellini quite rightly considers an occasion for group stupidity. This is precisely Fellini's point: Fascism allowed perfectly normal people during his childhood to behave in completely unpredictable and dangerous ways.

It is important to note that Fellini does not merely explain mass behavior during the Fascist period as a regressive state of adolescence. It is a regressive state of adolescence that finds its highest and most dangerous expression in sexual repression. All the Amarcordians find themselves in a state of high anxiety over sexual matters. Sexual innuendo fills their conversation and occupies their minds, yet the only kind of concrete sexual expression tolerated by Fascist culture is either within marriage, with the local prostitutes (brothels were regulated by the state at the time, and almost all Italian males had their first sexual experiences there), with the town nymphomaniac, Volpina, or with visiting Nordic tourists during the tourist season. Every other kind of sexual expression outside marriage is severely condemned, including adolescent masturbation, which the local priest attempts to stamp out via the confessional, without success. Guilt accompanies sex at every stage of an Amarcordian's existence.

Ultimately, Fellini sees a causal connection between the repressed sexuality of his childhood, the Fascist culture of mass psychosis demonstrated during the *federale*'s visit, and the way the townspeople experience the cinema and its American myths as a source of relief from their tedious and provincial lives. The link of repressed sexuality and Fascism is made abundantly clear when Gradisca (Magali Noël), the object of desire for the entire town, goes into ecstasy over the very sight of the visiting Fascist dignitary. When Mussolini addressed a large crowd in his heyday, it was frequently reported that women left wet underpants in the square, so sexually excited were they by his speeches and his personal charisma. Unbelievable as it may seem now, it was even common practice for Italian men to attend such rallies in order to meet women who were already in a state of sexual arousal! Gradisca responds to the *federale* exactly as a woman might respond to a lover. When Lallo, dressed in his black Fascist uniform, chimes in after the mathematics professor's remarks in the parade, his comment is a crude sexual summation of this attitude: "All I can say is . . . Mussolini's got two balls this big!"[18]

To underscore the connection between a misguided sexuality and the political regime that fostered such a prolonged state of adolescence, Fellini offers another example of this linkage during Gradisca's encounter with the passing ocean liner *Rex,* another excuse for the Amarcordians to gather together to demonstrate their immaturity. The entire town sails out into the Adriatic, hoping to catch a glimpse of the proud symbol of the regime. These shots in the actual ocean suddenly turn into a studio location, where obviously fake boats rock back and forth on an obviously fake ocean, produced by sheets of black plastic. When the ocean liner finally appears, it is an artificial studio creation, a fake cardboard ship with backlighting in its portholes that was erected at Cinecittà and actually stood abandoned on the lot there for many years after the film was completed until it rotted away from rain and wind. Once again, Gradisca becomes almost hysterical in her desire to reach out toward the ship, just as she had passionately desired to touch the visiting *federale* physically during the parade. After its passing, the townspeople fail to notice that the *Rex* is merely a flat façade that falls back into the ocean, revealing its status as both a movie prop and the embodiment of a false and mystifying image manipulated by an evil regime; but Fellini's film audience should grasp the message immediately.

For all his love of the cinema, Fellini believes that the repressed lives of the Amarcordians relied far too heavily upon the facile and superficial myths delivered weekly by the local movie theater, the Cinema Fulgor. Thus, before the sequence of the town parade for the *federale,* Fellini inserts two important sequences that help to explain why the townspeople react as they do to the regime's political symbols. In the first sequence, Titta and his friends go to confession, where the priest is solely concerned with whether the boys "touch themselves." The effect of the priest's questioning about masturbation has quite the op-

Titta (Bruno Zanin) unsuccessfully attempts to seduce Gradisca (Magali Nöel) in the Cinema Fulgor. [*Photo:* The Museum of Modern Art/Film Stills Archive]

posite result expected, for Titta begins to ask himself how it would be possible not to touch oneself with so many images of ripe womanhood around him – Volpina, the math professor, plump peasant women with enormous bottoms, and most particularly Gradisca. Within Titta's fantasy as he makes his confession (or at least pretends to do so), Titta narrates his encounter with Gradisca one afternoon as she was watching Gary Cooper in *Beau Geste,* smoking alone in the theater. Gradisca sits entranced, in an obvious state of aroused sexual awareness brought about by the image of the American actor. Titta enters the theater and moves closer and closer to Gradisca, finally placing his hand upon her leg. He is then devastated by her crushing remark when she breaks out of her trance and finally perceives his presence: "Looking for something?"

Fellini's point is that the mechanism that attracts Gradisca to Gary Cooper is not unlike the mechanism that attracts the crowd to the *fede-*

rale or to the *Rex,* symbols of the Fascist regime. Unhealthy sexuality can be expressed only in an unhealthy fashion, and such bottled-up energy can be channeled into potentially dangerous directions by a regime with expertise in manipulating symbols of a certain kind. Unrequited sexual desire and its repression by either the church or the state have extremely negative consequences. In Titta's case, his encounter with an enormous woman who sells cigarettes in the town provides one of the most hilarious moments of the film. He declares he is strong enough to lift this huge female, she challenges him to do so, and when Titta barely manages to lift her, she suddenly is carried away by a momentary fit of sexual passion and gives the young man her enormous breast to suck under a De Chirico–like poster of Dante with his brain exposed hanging on the wall (an advertisement). The shock of this encounter is so great that Titta takes to his bed, and his mother is forced to try to revive his energies with mustard plasters. An even more extreme example of how sexual repression can destroy a person's sanity is then provided by the family's visit to the local asylum to visit Uncle Teo, who climbs to the top of a huge tree and screams over and over, "I want a woman!" His cry might well be the motto of the entire male population of *Amarcord,* and it is not by accident that only a dwarf nun can bring Teo down from his perch, underlining the ultimate origin of this grotesque behavior and its source in sexual repression sponsored by the church.

To this point, our discussion of *Amarcord* has stressed the very significant ideas Fellini has about politics and the Fascist regime that underpin his narrative and motivate his imagery. It is important to highlight two facts about this wonderful film that are often overlooked. In the first place, the political "message" of *Amarcord,* if its interpretation of Italian Fascism as a state of arrested psychological development can be called such, is delivered not with the pompous rhetoric of the ideologue but with the exquisite imagery of a poet. The almost universal popularity of this film can only be explained by its visual power and not its thematic content. Like *La dolce vita, Amarcord* presents us with countless moments of great beauty and emotional appeal, even when the subject matter is not always so gratifying. It would be impossible to discuss them all, but a few examples will serve to demonstrate that Fellini's greatest "political" film is really one of his greatest "poetic" films. The sequences dealing with the visiting *federale,* the passage of the *Rex,* or Titta's encounter with Gradisca are not only important ve-

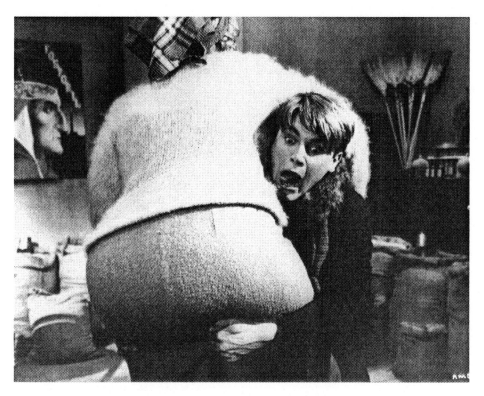

Titta (Bruno Zanin) tries to lift the enormous tobacconist (Maria Antonietta Beluzzi). [*Photo:* The Museum of Modern Art/Film Stills Archive]

hicles for carrying forward Fellini's arguments about how political ideology and cinematic myths operate upon our psyches, but they are also some of the most hilarious and beautiful metacinematic moments in the work. Titta approaches Gradisca in a movie theater; the *Rex* is a movie prop; and the Fascist visits what a careful observer will perceive as the major buildings of Cinecittà! Fellini used the Fascist-style movie studio as a ready-made prop, since its architecture (created as one of the Fascist regime's showplaces) was so typical of the regime's architectural style that he required very few props to complete the sequence. While the main argument of these three sequences concerns the link between personal behavior and mass behavior, the subtext of them all remains the cinema. In spite of Fellini's obvious distaste for the political regime governing the Amarcordians or the closed society that produced its sex-

Young Italians dream of an ideal Fascist marriage before a bust of Mussolini in a fantasy sequence of *Amarcord*. [*Photo:* The Museum of Modern Art/Film Stills Archive]

ual repression and its cultural emptiness, once again the director cannot help but reproduce the memory of his past in beautiful, striking images. The appearance of the beautiful peacock in the snow entrances not only the townspeople but also Fellini's audience. Its almost magic arrival on the screen cannot but help to recall the equally magic and evocative appearance of the magicians or the horse in *La strada* or any number of similar surrealistic apparitions in other works. Still, this beautiful bird as it spreads it gossamer wings also serves as a harsh commentary on the life of the town, for the peacock has always served as the archetypal image of vanity and dangerous self-centeredness in Italian culture since the Middle Ages. Equally ambivalent are Fellini's caricature portraits of the entire town. Fascists resemble *august* (stupid grotesque) clowns, townspeople recall cartoon characters. While we can see the deleterious effects of the actions of such characters, their comic qualities also make us laugh and even forgive them their faults. Like Fellini, Fellini's audience slowly changes from witnesses for the prosecution to witnesses for the defense. Fellini's art is always a comic art, and that implies acceptance, understanding, even empathy, rather than mere criticism and exorcism of evil.

Thus, Fellini produces an important statement about politics and Italian political history with poetic images, not rhetorical speeches or ideological narratives. If his "political" film reflects his "poetic" style, however, it is also not merely autobiographical as some interpretations of *Amarcord* have claimed. The wonderfully evocative explanation of Gradisca's name is a perfect case in point. As Dario Zanelli has noted, in *Amarcord*, Gradisca supposedly received her name because she was brought to the Grand Hotel to sleep with a visiting prince in order to help the town receive funding for the harbor: When she invited the prince to enter her bed, she offered her body to him with the phrase "Gradisca" (meaning "Please do" or "Help yourself!"). In fact, Zanelli located the historic Gradisca and discovered that her name came from a place where her father was fighting on the Austrian–Italian frontier during the time of her birth, November 1915! Titta's own narration of his friendship with Fellini underscores how many of the so-called biographical events in *Amarcord* (like those in *8 1/2*) are often fictitious inventions of Fellini's imaginative fantasy. As the director has quite rightly stated, "my films from my past recount memories that are completely invented."[19] In spite of writing his memoirs about his adolescence in

Rimini and discussing many of the people who become his characters in *Amarcord*, Fellini refuses to consider his works autobiographical, rejecting a reductionist explanation of his life. Particularly in regard to *Amarcord*, Fellini finds explaining his art by his biography offensive:

> I'm always a bit offended when I hear that one of my films is "auto-biographical": it seems like a reductionist definition to me, especially if then, as it often happens, "autobiographical" comes to be understood in the sense of anecdotal, like someone who tells old school stories.[20]

Yet, Fellini also realizes that fact and fiction have become so completely intertwined in his mind that he can no longer separate them:

> Now I can't distinguish what really happened from what I made up. Superimposed on my real memories are painted memories of a plastic sea, and characters from my adolescence in Rimini are elbowed aside by actors or extras who interpreted them in my films.[21]

While Zanelli's research into Fellini's past reveals that his characters in *Amarcord* are produced primarily by his fertile fantasy, as in the case of Gradisca's name, Fellini himself repeated the invented story of the prince in the Grand Hotel in his autobiographical essay "My Rimini," and the tale has become so popular that it is almost impossible to convince Fellini's fans that the invented story is not the true explanation.

Fellini has frequently declared that he is a puppet master, a complete inventor of everything about his life and his art:

> I'm a liar, but an honest one. People reproach me for not always telling the same story in the same way. But this happens because I've invented the whole tale from the start and it seems boring to me and unkind to other people to repeat myself.[22]

If Fellini's cinematic art rests upon such "lies," perhaps it is useful to recall Picasso's famous definition of art as a lie that tells the truth.

6

Intervista

A Summation of a Cinematic Career

Fellini's penultimate feature film, *Intervista* [Interview] (1987), was awarded prizes at the Moscow International Film Festival and at the fortieth anniversary of the Cannes Film Festival. Unlike most of Fellini's previous works, *Intervista* was not based upon a highly polished literary script. In past films, even those that seemed to contain improvised sequences, such as parts of *8 ½*, *Block-notes di un regista*, *I clowns*, or *Roma*, Fellini worked from a polished script that was the result of long and patient collaboration with a number of writers. In the case of *Intervista*, however, Fellini relied upon a loosely constructed series of sketches, ideas, or notepads (*block-notes*, as they are called in Italian) that outlined a skeletal idea for four projected television programs, all based upon Fellini's memories from the past or his impressions of four themes that had intrigued him throughout his long career.

The four themes initially identified as the subject of these television programs were as follows: Italian opera; the Cinema Fulgor in Rimini; Cinecittà; and America. Very little of this material finally entered the completed film *Intervista*. In fact, Fellini has always declared that he dislikes music in general, opera in particular, even though Nino Rota's musical scores for his works have become famous. He was well known for paying itinerant musicians visiting Roman restaurants *not* to perform. Fellini has always admitted to knowing little or nothing about America, although the country had always fascinated him since his childhood, both because of the American film and cartoon and also because America liberated Italy from the odious Fascist regime that Fellini despised. Since a number of his previous works contained material on the Cinema Fulgor (*Block-notes di un regista, Roma, Amarcord*), by a process of elimination Fellini was left with his devotion to Cinecittà as a possible storyline for what would become a film after the television projects were abandoned.

Even the Italian script of *Intervista* that was eventually published was not the reflection of a previously existing literary script that served as the basis for Fellini's work on the set when *Intervista* was finally shot. Instead, the published script we have comes from a moviola analysis of the completed film after work on the set was concluded. Fellini described the final product in several ways. In an introduction to the published Italian script, he defined the work as a "little film" (a *filmetto*).[1] In an interview with Dario Zanelli, Fellini spoke of *Intervista* as a "live" film (*un film in diretto*) "that unfolds as you watch it," employing the term now used by the medium (television) he had always claimed to despise to underline his film's spontaneous, unpretentious nature. Moreover, he referred to *Intervista* as "this pleasant chat among friends" that represented the final stage in the evolution of his cinematic style, "where there is no longer a story or a script" and only "the feeling . . . of being inside a kind of creativity that refuses every preconceived order."[2] The film's simple charm derives from the fact that *Intervista* is as close to a spontaneous work of art, produced under the very eyes of its audience, as could be possible to achieve in the highly sophisticated and technical art that is the cinema.

Gianfranco Angelucci, former director of Rimini's Federico Fellini Foundation and the scriptwriter who collaborated with Fellini to create *Intervista,* has called the film a "lighter *8 1/2*." He has explained the film's genesis by a useful comparison to the world of Renaissance art, describing Fellini as a Renaissance master fresco artist who, inspired by the wisdom that only comes with maturity, ultimately rejects the more complicated but traditional painting of a narrative fresco. Instead, he concentrates upon a series of loosely related preparatory drawings, not unlike those created by painters such as Leonardo da Vinci, the kind of minimal art that reveals more about the *process* of artistic creation than about a traditional narrative.[3] The preparatory drawings of the great European masters of the Renaissance and beyond serve art historians or museumgoers today as invaluable clues in deciphering how a completed work is conceived, worked out, and completed. Ultimately, like the sketches of such artists, Fellini's sketchbooks and loosely related ideas about Cinecittà in *Intervista* serve him in a similar manner.

Intervista was thus conceived to fulfill a number of interrelated purposes. Produced in 1987, *Intervista* represented Fellini's tribute to what he had always called the place where he truly came alive – the enormous Cinecittà studio complex on the outskirts of the city of Rome that contains Teatro 5 (renamed Studio Fellini after the director's death), Europe's largest sound theater. Fellini produced his most important works, with few exceptions, within this studio complex, and it was only natural that as the individual most often identified with this institution in the postwar period, Fellini would join in the celebration of Cinecittà's fiftieth anniversary after its inauguration by the Italian Fascist government on 21 April 1937. While frequently satirizing the Fascist regime's fixation with this mythical date of the foundation of Rome (this is the same day on which the *federale* visits the provincial town in *Amarcord*), Fellini and everyone else in the international motion picture business have always acknowledged the debt they owed to Mussolini for at least this one beneficial state intervention in Italian culture. *Intervista* also represented a summation of Fellini's views on the nature of the cinema itself, on its craft, and on its future. Such a preoccupation with the nature of the cinema itself was brilliantly treated in *8 1/2* and also, to a lesser extent, in the earlier *Block-notes di un regista* and the subsequent *Roma* and *E la nave va*. This theoretical interest in discussing the nature of the cinema entails, of necessity, some treatment of Fellini's own biography, and as a result *Intervista* also provided a nostalgic look back to Fellini's first encounter with the studio that was Italy's Hollywood.

As Angelucci has noted, *Intervista* must be viewed against the background of *8 1/2*. Its plot reminds the viewer immediately of that earlier masterpiece as well as of *Block-notes di un regista*.[4] *8 1/2* focuses upon a creative crisis in the life of a film director named Guido Anselmi, who is played by the actor frequently identified as Fellini's alter ego, Marcello Mastroianni. *Intervista* is also about a film director, but in it Fellini plays himself and employs no alter ego. Mastroianni appears again in *Intervista*, but for an entirely different purpose than that of *8 1/2*, where he mediated between the director Fellini and his representation by an actor on the screen. Whereas Fellini's alter ego Guido experienced the depths of an artistic block in *8 1/2* and lived through a personal crisis, in *Intervista* Fellini feels no need for an actor to mediate between him and the audience. He plays himself and creates a film before the audience's eyes as effortlessly as he breathes and walks. Indeed, in *Intervista,* making a film represents a metaphor for the creative process and becomes synonymous with life itself.

The earlier *8 1/2* was filled with press conferences and imaginary interviews, and it is precisely following a press conference that Guido surmounts his creative blockage and plunges into the moving finale of the work. One of the important themes of *Intervista,* as its title implies, is the interview itself. There are, in fact, not one but two interviews in the film. The first is of Fellini himself, done by a Japanese television crew at Cinecittà. This provides Fellini with the pretense not only to grant an interview but to parody one as well. The second interview in the film links the past to the present, for Fellini is moved by his conversation with the Japanese to recount his own autobiographical reminiscences of his first visit to the studio complex in 1940. Fellini actually first visited Cinecittà not as a scriptwriter, an actor, or a director but as a timid young journalist who had been assigned to interview a beautiful and famous actress shooting a film there.

In *8 1/2,* Guido tried to complete a science-fiction film but failed; Fellini's completed film was, in fact, the narration of Guido's *incomplete* film. In *Intervista,* Fellini pretends to prepare for the making of an ambitious historical film, an adaptation of Franz Kafka's *Amerika* that leads him to select actors and actresses for the various roles, to study historical photographs of America during the time Kafka set his story in the United States, and to design lavish sets for the film. A fictitious production thus provides Fellini with the excuse to be on the set of Cinecittà. Reminiscent of *8 1/2,* we see a number of possible actresses to play a single role, that of a buxom prostitute in a bordello. *8 1/2* and *Intervista* thus both contain two other films never destined for completion, as well as the screen tests for the films that will forever remain incomplete.

Intervista actually contains three *potential* films, each one of which is constantly intertwined with the other two during the course of the narrative. The spectator is given glimpses of various parts of each of these films but is never permitted to see any one of them in a completed form. In effect, they are fragmented by being constantly interrupted by each other. The first *potential* film is a documentary (or parody of a documentary) made by Japanese journalists about Fellini at Cinecittà. Given Fellini's distaste for realism or naturalism in the cinema, there is little chance that this particular theme will ever be realized fully other than as a parody of the possibilities of recording "reality" in a documentary context. Since the Asian journalists naturally ask Fellini about his past, the first documentary film leads logically into a second *potential* film, in which Fellini responds by illustrating his first experiences at Cinecittà as a young journalist. Unlike the documentary, where Fellini appears as himself being interviewed by reporters, the second possible film involves a far more complex story with a young actor (Sergio Rubini) playing the youthful Fellini. Moreover, this particular film in the making also involves a relatively complex series of sets, costumes, and historical locations in order to reproduce the Cinecittà of 1940. It is also more complex in its metacinematic dimension, since the spectator sees both the production of these scenes from Fellini's memory as well as some of the final product of the film that would have been completed. In other words, the viewer sees work behind the camera as well as sequences that are actually shot. Finally, the third *potential* film is the adaptation of Kafka's *Amerika* that Fellini supposedly is preparing at the very moment the Japanese visit him. Like the second film, this, too, involves a greater level of complexity and requires screen tests, elaborate costumes, and historical study of America during the epoch in which Kafka's novel was set.

Even more than *8 1/2*, *Intervista* thus reflects a Chinese-box kind of construction where a number of potential films are all contained in a fourth, *realized* film that is actually created in its totality, unlike the three *potential* films that are enclosed within the fourth film and are, by definition, always destined to remain incomplete. This fourth, actualized film is, precisely and paradoxically, *Intervista*, the film Fellini creates before our very eyes and that chronicles the visit of the Japanese journalists, Fellini's memories of his distant past at the studio, and his temptation to adapt Kafka's novel for the silver screen.

Naturally, this kind of narrative structure calls immediately to mind *8 1/2*, but there is a fundamental difference between the two works. In the earlier film, Fellini had been hesitant to interject himself into the narrative. Marcello Mastroianni played his alter ego, Guido Anselmi, and Fellini's actual presence in the film is felt primarily at the end of the work, where Guido joins the magic procession in the circus ring, the camera draws back, and we are presented with a point of view that can only be that of the director of *8 1/2*, Federico Fellini. Both *8 1/2* and *Intervista* reflect Fellini's belief that cinematic art, founded upon the irrational and the subconscious and privileging the emotions, provides a way of knowing for humankind that represents as valid an epistemology as philosophical, logical, or ideological types of intellectual discourse. Now in *Intervista*, Fellini wants to emphasize that an artist committed to this kind of discourse really *lives* the cinema and does not merely work within it. Creativity is a natural, healthy human talent, and by presenting the viewer with a film seemingly produced under his or her nose, Fellini wants his audience to experience the kinds of emotions that normally could be possible only by being physically present on the set with him. In other words, whereas *8 1/2* was primarily a manifesto about the nature of the intellectual experience that goes into the creation of art, *Intervista* is primarily a manifesto about the *craft* that goes into actualizing that kind of artistic creation.

The emphasis on the craft of filmmaking involves revealing the illusionist elements of the cinema directors employ in producing films that convince the audience that what they are watching is *mimetic* – that is, a representation of reality. Fellini both reveals the illusions and simultaneously obscures them.[5] For example, we are constantly shown works in progress during the course of the film – sets being constructed, models being built, costumes being sewn, actors being made up, screen tests being conducted. This revelation of the craft of filmmaking underscores its artificiality, its illusionist character. Subsequently, these same sets, models, costumes, and actors are set within a sequence of a "real" film – that is, of a section of the film entitled *Intervista* that at least pretends, for a moment, to present a sequence meant to be viewed by us, its audience, as a believable fiction. The movements in the film back and forth between revelations of the medium and expressions of the medium's powers of persuasion are quite remarkable. Although *8 1/2* does contain moments of self-reflexivity, the self-reflexivity of *Intervista* is far more radical because it underlines the extradiegetic, offscreen space we would see if we were actually on the set, watching Fellini at work; thus, the revelation of the medium in *Intervista*, unlike in *8 1/2*, stresses the director's limitations.[6] Fellini pictures himself as constrained to employ the instruments of representation, even though he would clearly prefer to create ex nihilo in a cinematic stream of consciousness without recourse to such techniques of his craft.

Numerous examples of this ambivalent attitude toward the technical aspects of the cinema abound in *Intervista*. Most of the sequences that represent this theme in the film have a connection with Fellini's recollections of his first visit to Cinecittà in 1940. First, he is questioned by the Japanese journalists about his past while he is busy setting up an enormous crane for what he claims will be a shot over the entire establishment of Cinecittà from the rooftop level. In this scene, which opens the film without any credits to announce that the film has begun, we are shown not only the rather primitive equipment of the journalists but also the much more sophisticated camera and crane employed by Fellini's director of photography, Tonino Delli Colli. Fellini claims to his interlocutors that he thought about beginning the film with a dream sequence, something he admits he has done earlier (his reference is to the opening of *8 1/2*). At the end of the sequence, assisted by a lunar light typical of photography in space and the magical smoke made from various chemicals that Fellini always employed to suggest a dreamlike, ethereal atmosphere, the film rolls on in silence as the enormous crane is shot against the background of the smoke and light. It is one of the most beautiful shots in the film, and a moment later, Fellini stages his dream sequence, which portrays his hand moving on a wall in a dark room as if in a dream. Seeing the roofs of a mysterious structure, on the voice-over Fellini tries to identify his surroundings:

> I found myself in a dark and troublesome environment, but one that was at the same time also familiar . . . the darkness was profound . . . and my hands touched a wall that never ended. In other films, in dreams like this one, I freed myself by flying away, but now who knows, a little older and a little heavier, I lifted myself from the ground with great difficulty. . . . Finally I succeeded, and I found myself freed at a great height, and the landscape I saw through pieces of clouds, down there on the ground, what was it? The university campus, the hospital . . . it looked like a penitentiary, an atomic bomb shelter. . . . Finally, I recognized it, and it was Cinecittà.[7]

With the dramatic realization of the magical appearance of Cinecittà, Fellini seems to have revealed to the spectator something of the craft

Fellini directs the photography of the scale model of Rome's Cinecittà, the enormous studio complex outside the city that is the true star of *Intervista*. [*Photo:* Federico Fellini and Studio Longardi (Rome)]

149

of his trade – the use of an enormous crane to capture the sensation of flying in a dream over the rooftops of Italy's Hollywood. Later in the film, after a bomb scare empties one of the many studio workshops, while the police investigate who might have made the telephone call alerting the film crew to a possible terrorist attack, the real mystery sits in front of the attentive viewer's eyes: It is the scale model of Cinecittà that has actually been employed in the film's opening sequences. Thus, while Fellini showed the spectator an opening sequence containing the magical crane to convince us that he was really employing such a technique to represent the studio, in fact he had produced the dreamlike appearance of the studio with a simple model fabricated by some of the studio's master carpenters. He has therefore both revealed the artifice of his craft and falsified it, as well.

This tendency both to reveal and to obscure the artifice of filmmaking continues and becomes the dominant theme of Fellini's re-creation of his actual visit to the studio on the trolley that used to depart, years ago, from the Casa del Passeggero in downtown Rome. First of all, Fellini's crew goes to the actual location of the Casa but discovers that it is too dilapidated to use now after years of neglect. They also visit the depository of the city transportation system to inspect the remaining trolley cars still used in Rome. Naturally, as in his other films, Fellini finds the "real" locations insufficient for his artistic intentions, just as he had done on a much larger scale in such works as *La dolce vita* or *8 1/2*, and his habitual decision to create illusionist sets of real places follows. A perfectly plausible set for the Casa is produced by adding a few touches to another similar building, while the trolley that will take the actor playing the young Fellini is constructed by cutting a single trolley into two parts to provide the camera crew with a space to work in each section, creating the illusion that shots inside the car actually take place inside a whole carriage. Mounting the two pieces upon the bed of a large truck enables Fellini to create the illusion of motion (not unlike the way he placed the entire bridge of an ocean liner on a movable structure in *E la nave va* to create the rocking motion of the ocean's waves). We are first shown the artifice of the sequence that is to follow – the young Fellini's trolley trip out to the studio to interview an actress – and then we are returned to a "realistic" depiction of the trolley trip. However, Fellini's re-creation of the distance his younger self travels stretches across not only distance but also the imagination.

Along the way, we see elephants typical of the kinds of jungle movie that were shot during the prewar era; there are magical waterfalls that could never be found around the outskirts of Rome; a tribe of American Indians presents itself menacingly as if to attack the trolley as if it were a stagecoach in a John Ford western; and the car makes one stop to greet a group of singing peasants who have just harvested the year's grape crop. When the trolley reaches the actual entrance to the Cinecittà establishment, the momentary trip into the past (and into a mimetic representation of the past) is fractured immediately with the appearance of the adult Fellini, who continues to recount how he first arrived at the studio for his interview. As one critic puts it, Fellini's constant shifting between illusionism and self-reflexivity in *Intervista* raises the typical postmodern epistemological doubts about knowledge and suggests that how we know takes place only through "arbitrary, provisional, and ultimately unstable" codes.[8] In other words, Fellini's playful treatment of the traditional codes of illusionist cinema so normal in the conventional commercial film is juxtaposed to the newer but still codified rules of self-reflexive cinema typical of the "art" film or the film modernism of a work such as *8 1/2*. The conclusion the spectator may draw from these different aesthetic codes is that rather than there really being a language of the cinema, there are many such languages, but none of them enjoys any privileged relationship to "reality." Reality itself is a code, a convention, a set of aesthetic rules that may easily be broken, revised, revealed, or ignored, as the director desires.

Fellini thus plays with almost every kind of code or rule in *Intervista*, including the traditional and most conventional codes of the commercial cinema, those linked to mimetic representation of "reality." However, playing with these codes, satirizing them, or parodying them does not necessarily entail rejecting them all, as is evident from an examination of one crucial feature of *Intervista* – the image of the film director. There are a number of film directors shown to the audience in *Intervista*. Besides Fellini himself and Sergio Rubini, who plays the young Fellini in 1940, there are at least four other director figures: Two are shown shooting two different films outside the buildings of Cinecittà in 1940, and two others are filming television commercials, also on the studio grounds, during the year *Intervista* was being shot (1987). In spite of the very different epochs and artistic media involved (1940, 1987; traditional cinema and television), the image of the direc-

tor remains constant. When Rubini/Fellini enters the studio grounds, he walks into a scene directed by a man resembling Alessandro Blasetti, one of the most important directors of the prewar period. The scene to be filmed involves two soon-to-be married people in love running together in an embrace, almost the archetypal target of any parody of a love scene. The scene is shot several times, causing the autocratic director to climb down from his perch high above the location to demonstrate himself how the embrace should be effected. To make the scene even more comic, the director embraces the groom more passionately than the bride. His dictatorial nature is underlined by the fact that he

Fellini re-creates the kind of lavish historical set typical of films of the 1940s, the period when he first visited Cinecittà. [*Photo:* The Museum of Modern Art / Film Stills Archive]

makes a completely ridiculous request for a pear (precisely the only fruit not available) during a break in the shooting, as if to underline his authoritarian character.

When Rubini/Fellini interviews the movie star about to perform in a scene set in India during the British Raj, he enters Studio 14, where the sound stage has been decorated as if it were a location in the kind of exotic East imagined by so many adventure films in the prewar period. Here, we are treated to a glimpse into the kind of historical costume drama so popular in the history of the cinema, exactly the kind of film Fellini usually avoided making at all costs during his career. We meet the producer, a man trying desperately to save money by refusing to provide real elephants for the scene, forcing the production crew to use its ingenuity by constructing papier-mâché reproductions of elephants. At one point during the shooting, one of the false elephant trunks falls on the floor, provoking the director to break into a hysterical fit of anger, threatening to go to Germany where real money is given to artists. At the height of his anger, he knocks over an entire row of fake elephants. Fellini clearly believes that such a dictatorial attitude is a natural requirement of the director's personality. He demonstrates this belief by stepping into the very scene where the fictitious film director knocks down the fake elephants: Unsatisfied with the way the scene has been performed, and parallel to the dissatisfaction both fictitious directors from the 1940s have exhibited on both sets, Fellini demonstrates how the scene should be played, knocking over the rest of the fake elephants.

Even though Fellini has little positive to say about television, he briefly depicts two directors working in that medium who both possess the same kind of authoritarian personalities as the directors working in the cinema. On the lot of Cinecittà and in the same spot where in 1940 Rubini/Fellini witnesses the fit of anger of the first film director, television commercials for Imperial typewriters and a brand of lipstick (among other things) are being filmed. Briefly, the director of one commercial reacts just as negatively and as angrily to the results of his work as did both film directors decades earlier. Later, when Marcello Mastroianni appears dressed as Mandrake the Magician and working in a commercial for laundry detergent – joking about how this is the only kind of work he can find – we see another scene in which yet another television commercial director, played by the scriptwriter Gianfranco Angelucci, is showing fake housewives how to celebrate the qualities of the soap he is helping to sell. In this case, the fact that Angelucci is playing a director of commercials is actually an in-joke, for besides working with Fellini for many years, at the time *Intervista* was being shot, Angelucci was actually one of the owners of Studio 54, a firm with an office at Cinecittà. In that capacity, Angelucci made several very famous commercials for Italian television. He was, therefore, a "real" director of television commercials, and unlike the other three director figures, Angelucci's presence in *Intervista* reveals a "real" performance, not a "fake" performance of actors pretending to be directors.

Stepping into the scene that re-creates a film director's tirade during the 1940s, Fellini shows the actor playing the director how to play the scene and when the fake elephants should be knocked over. [*Photo:* Studio Longardi (Rome)]

As a social institution and an artistic medium, television represents the antithesis of what Fellini believes to be the essence of the cinema. Even though he had himself made films for television (including *Block-notes di un regista* for the American National Broadcasting Company and *I clowns* for the Italian public network, the RAI), as well as a number of television commercials for Barilla pasta, Campari aperitif, and the Bank of Rome, there are a number of traits typical of television that set it apart from the cinema, at least the kind of personal, poetic cinema always identified with Fellini's career. Fellini's critique of television involved a number of qualities he saw as being antithetical to film defined as the product of an auteur, an individual artist. In the first place, as Fellini noted as early as 1969–70 during the production of *Block-notes di un regista* and *I clowns,* the language of television involves a diminution of the possibilities of the language of the cinema: The small screen requires close-ups rather than extra-long shots and basically a homogenization of the artistic achievements made by the cinema over a period of years. Moreover, Fellini believed television was a medium best suited for the communication of information rather than the expression of an artistic vision. As Fellini's thinking evolved and the director's thoughts on television moved him to shoot *Ginger e Fred,* a film about the role of this medium in the contemporary world, other criticisms were added to those made earlier. Between 1969 and the production of *Ginger e Fred,* television's impact upon Italian society had dramatically increased, while the dominant role played by traditional cinema within Italian popular culture had been seriously compromised by a crisis in the industry, foreign competition, and the rise of television. During Fellini's formative prewar years, film and variety shows were the most important forms of popular entertainment. Although the variety theater began to disappear during the postwar period, the movie theater remained the focus of Italian popular culture from the end of the war until the mid-1970s. Besides the obvious drop in ticket sales that occurred after that time, Fellini was far more concerned about the atmosphere or context in which films were shown to an Italian public that been radically transformed since Fellini began work in the industry. Rather than going to a movie theater in a kind of public ritual, entering a dark moviehouse along with a group of like-minded spectators, and experiencing a communal form of artistic expression based upon the personal artistic fantasies of an individual director, Italians now began to see films primarily on television, all too often interrupted by jarring commercials. As a result, the personal communication between spectator and auteur, between dreamer and the producer of the dream, had all but evaporated:

> I, too, think that the cinema has lost authority, prestige, mystery, and magic. The giant screen that dominates an audience devotedly gathered in front of it no longer fascinates us. Once it dominated tiny little men staring enchanted at immense faces, lips, eyes, living and breathing in another unreachable dimension, fantastic and at the same time real, like a dream. Now we have learned to dominate it. We are bigger than it. . . . Sometimes it's [the television set] even in the kitchen, near the refrigerator. It has become an electric domestic servant and we, seated in armchairs, armed with remote control, exercise a total power over those little images, rejecting whatever is unfamiliar or boring to us. . . . What a bore that Bergman! Who said Buñuel was a great director? Out of the house with them. I want to see a ball game or a variety show. Thus a tyrant spectator is born,

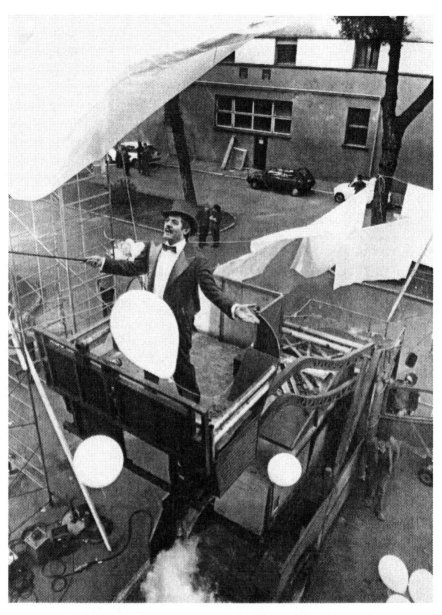

Marcello Mastroianni magically appears outside Fellini's office while he is shooting a television commercial on the lot of Cinecittà in *Intervista*. [*Photo:* The Museum of Modern Art / Film Stills Archive]

an absolute despot who does what he wants and is more and more convinced that he is the director or at least the producer of the images he sees. How could the cinema possibly try to attract that kind of audience?[9]

Television replaced the authoritarian director, the creator of the work of art, with the authoritarian viewer, who controlled everything with a remote-control device. Moreover, television replaced the ritualistic experience that represents the cinema's very essence and that permitted the director to immerse the spectator into a dreamlike state within a public space (the movie theater) with a private and overly restricted world, one smaller rather than larger than life. In addition, television reduced everything it presented to the same level of insignificance and replaced any relationship with "reality," no matter how problematic that term or relationship might be, with mere simulations of reality. Thus in *Ginger e Fred,* look-alikes of famous people – Ronald Reagan, Queen Elizabeth, Woody Allen, Bette Davis, and many others – constantly turn up in the television studio and on the air, and Fellini employed such figures to emphasize television's "profoundly anticultural operation" and its emphasis upon approximation: Television mimicked without success the cinema, reality, and history just as these figures mimicked the originals they simulated.[10]

In *Intervista,* Fellini presents a comic version of his earlier and far more trenchant critiques of television by having a group of American Indians, armed with spears shaped like television antennae, attack his film crew, forcing them to defend themselves like the members of a wagon train in a Hollywood western. Since the Indians are associated with television, they, too, are fake: After the sequence is shot, one of them asks in an obvious Roman accent if the scene went well; he then picks up the traditional Italian Christmas gift on a film set – a *panettone* and a bottle of *spumante!*

Fellini may well accept postmodern ideas about the fallacy of "realistic" representation in the cinema, playing with various cinematic or visual codes and satirizing their pretensions. He does this not because he has become a postmodernist but, rather, because he has always maintained the same theories about the inadequacy or the inappropriateness of the cinema as a medium designed solely to record or reflect "reality." In fact, his career in the cinema began with a critique of Italian neorealism's pretensions toward precisely that kind of mimesis and evolved toward quite the opposite kind of cinema, one that might best be characterized as modernist – a cinema based upon the personal vision of an individual artist that found its highest expression in $8\frac{1}{2}$. If *Intervista* seems to share some characteristics of postmodernism – particularly a healthy skepticism about art's ability to reproduce reality – there are few hints in *Intervista* that Fellini believes the place of the individual director, the dreamer who shares his fantasies with a collective audience, has radically changed.

In *Intervista*, Fellini certainly presents an image of the director that is both comical and authoritarian; but every single pronouncement he has ever made about the art of the cinema focuses upon the central and irreplaceable role of the artist, the director who creates. In *Intervista*, Fellini explains to the Japanese interviewers the same sentiment he expressed years earlier in an important collection of interviews:

> Film is a divine way of telling about life, of paralleling God the Father! No other profession lets you create a world that comes so close to the one we know, as well as to unknown, parallel, concentric ones. For me the ideal place . . . is Teatro 5 in Cinecittà when it's empty . . . a space to fill up, a world to create.[11]

In an important BBC documentary on his entire career, Fellini employed not the image of the *Deus artifex* but a more mundane one, describing his profession as "precisely a total, cynical vocation of puppet master."[12] Fellini has always declared that the only true realist is the visionary, the creative artist who invents and fantasizes, not the mere recorder of events.[13] Even more important, in connection with *Intervista*, Fellini declared that cinema is not an art form that employs a camera full of film to record reality outside its lens. On the contrary, when a film is produced – at least a film such as Fellini produces – "you only put yourself in front of the camera lens."[14] Film art grows out of a projected subjectivity, not a loss of self, as postmodern art would have it.

Fellini's position on artistic creativity remains fundamentally removed from the essence of postmodernism. In his postscript to *The Name of the Rose*, Umberto Eco has quite correctly defined postmodernism as "irony, metalinguistic play, enunciation squared." More concretely, Eco compares the postmodern spirit to a man who wants to tell a very sophisticated woman that he loves her but realizes that the phrase "I love you" has been employed so often that it has little meaning. Therefore, he employs a postmodern technique and declares: "As Barbara Cartland would put it, I love you," at the same time providing an ironic, postmodern commentary on tradition and also speaking of love in the process.[15] Postmodern works of art are often works constructed by pastiche and consisting of numerous and ironic citations of other works of art. Nonetheless, if Fellini's *Intervista* shares some superficial traits of postmodernism – his ironic view of his profession, his metacinematic content, his playful treatment of his entire career – it should never be forgotten that Fellini's irony, metacinematic play, and his filmic enunciation squared always focus upon himself, his subjectivity, and his own works of art, not those created by others. Not only does his treatment of the history of the cinema boil down to a personal memoir of his own experiences in the cinema (and very little else), but almost everything about *Intervista* reminds the spectator of Fellini's career. The music on the sound track represents a medley of famous Nino Rota tunes, assembled by Nicola Piovani, all of which refer our ear to earlier Fellini films. The appearance of Marcello Mastroianni in the film cannot but remind us of two of Fellini's greatest masterpieces (*La dolce vita, 8 1/2*), both films that portray Fellini's private life and secret fantasy world through Mastroianni as the director's alter ego. Even the usual postmodern citations of other works of art, in *Intervista,* refer to Fellini's other films. The most important example of Fellini's autocitation takes place when Fellini and Mastroianni visit Anita Ekberg's home outside Rome. Both actors have changed visibly since their memorable performance together in *La dolce vita*. Dressed as Mandrake the Magician, Mastroianni conjures up the famous Trevi Fountain scene from the film that made them both famous. Although the juxtaposition of their physical appearance in 1959 and that in 1987 underlines the inevitable ravages of time, there is little doubt that the magic of that scene remains intact. Life is short but art is long, this sequence seems to shout out, and such an aesthetic position is anything but postmodern in tone.

The finale of *Intervista* concludes with a complete negation of the image of the effaced, postmodern artist with which Fellini certainly toyed in the rest of the film. Instead, Fellini says simply that after shooting *Intervista,* he was reminded of one of his producers who, years ago during the making of *La dolce vita,* complained about Fellini's failure to provide viewers with a ray of hope, a ray metaphorically described as one of sunshine. "Give me at least a ray of sunshine," the producer would beg Fellini during his screenings of the daily rushes.[16] Fellini had earlier included this request in the opening sequence of *8 1/2*: As Guido receives his medical exam at the spa, his doctor asks him if he is making another film without hope.[17] Fellini's voice-over in *Intervista* now decides to respond to this traditional critique of his works: "A ray of sunshine? Well, I don't know, let's try."[18] At that moment, the lights in the mythical Teatro 5 are dimmed, leaving only one beam of light framed by a camera suspended in the darkness. A member of the crew enters the frame, signals a take with the traditional clapper board, and as the image freezes, the film credits that were never shown at the opening of the film now roll over the image of an artificial "ray of sunshine." Capturing a beam of light with his lens, Fellini underlines the raw material of filmmaking – light and image: "For me, in fact, the cinema is this – images. Light comes even before the theme, even before the actors selected for the various roles. Light is really everything. . . . The image is expressed with light."[19] This heroic image of a film director attempting to create something from nothing in an empty film studio cannot but help recall the definition of God in the Creation Story of Genesis, the divine   who brings the universe into existence by creating it ex nihilo from the primordial substance of light – the same light that for Fellini represents the primal matter of the cinema.

Notes

Introduction

1. Cited from the sound track of *Real Dreams: Into the Dark with Federico Fellini* (BBC Omnibus Program Italian script MS), p. 2 (author's translation). I am grateful to Gianfranco Angelucci for providing me with the text of the program as well as a videotape of it.

2. The most curious document in the history of Fellini criticism is probably Frank Burke's *Fellini's Films: From Postwar to Postmodern* (New York: Twayne, 1996), which both accepts most of the ideological baggage of recent film theory and then attempts to redeem Fellini from a position of theoretical marginalization by a vain attempt to apply these same theoretical categories to Fellini's work. Contemporary critical categories of race, class, gender, or other sociological approaches to Fellini's cinema have limited explanatory value for a very simple reason: Fellini's cinema is fundamentally not concerned about the issues upon which contemporary theory fixates. To attempt to force Fellini's cinema into directions that are fundamentally alien to its intentions is doomed to failure.

Chapter 1. Federico Fellini: A Life in Cinema

1. In addition to the four awards for Best Foreign Film, Fellini won three Oscars for Best Costume Design (by Piero Gherardi for *La dolce vita* in 1961 and *8 ½* in 1963; by Danilo Donati for *Il Casanova di Fellini* in 1976). He received sixteen unsuccessful Oscar nominations in the following categories: three nominations for Best Original Screenplay (for Roberto Rossellini's *Roma, città aperta* in 1946; for *La strada* in 1956; and for

Amarcord in 1975); four nominations for Best Story and Screenplay (for Rossellini's *Paisà* in 1946; for *I vitelloni* in 1957; for *La dolce vita* in 1961; and for *8 ½* in 1963); one for Best Screenplay from Another Medium (for *Il Casanova di Fellini* in 1976); four for Best Director (for *La dolce vita* in 1961; for *8 ½* in 1963; for *Satyricon* in 1970; and for *Amarcord* in 1975); two nominations for Best Art and Set Direction (for *La dolce vita* in 1961 and for *8 ½* in 1963); one each for Best Costume Design and for Best Color (both for *Giulietta degli spiriti* in 1966).

2. The tally of the votes was as follows: Fellini (45), Welles (42), Kurosawa (32), Coppola (26), Scorsese (23), Buñuel (23), Bergman (22), Chaplin (21), Ford (21), Hitchcock (21). This 1992 poll reveals a great deal about the state of film criticism and film theory in the English-speaking world, for while those actually working in the industry ranked Fellini at the top of the list, one hundred film critics around the world were far more predictable in their tastes, omitting Fellini entirely from their Top Ten List and giving the laurel leaf to the traditional winner, Welles, followed by Renoir, Godard, Hitchcock, Chaplin, Ford, Ray, Ozu, Dreyer, and Eisenstein. It is the contention of this book that this enormous disparity between the estimation of film directors and film critics says more about the prejudices and blind spots of the critics than it does about Fellini's actual significance or his contributions to the art of the movies. Of course, such ranking contests have nothing to do with art, as Fellini himself was very well aware. He once declared: "I'm not a man who approves of definitions. Labels belong on luggage as far as I'm concerned; they don't mean anything in art" (cited by Suzanne Budgen, *Fellini* [London: British Film Institute, 1966], p. 92). For a brief history of Fellini criticism, see Peter Bondanella and Cristina Degli-Esposti, "Federico Fellini: A Brief Overview of the Critical Literature," in Bondanella and Degli-Esposti, eds., *Perspectives on Federico Fellini* (New York: G. K. Hall/Maxwell Macmillan Intl., 1993), pp. 3–21.

3. Federico Fellini, *Fellini on Fellini*, ed. Anna Keel and Christian Strich, trans. Isabel Quigley (New York: Da Capo Press, 1996; rpt. of the original English edition [London: Eyre Methuen, 1976]), pp. 5, 6; Federico Fellini, *La mia Rimini* (Bologna: Capelli, 1987; original edition 1967), p. 30. For an interesting discussion of the role Rimini has played in the history of the cinema, including Fellini's works, see the catalog to the exhibit devoted to this topic at the Centre Georges Pompidou in Paris in 1989: Gianfranco Miro Gori, ed., *Rimini e le cinéma: images, cinéastes, histoires* (Paris: Éditions du Centre Georges Pompidou, 1989). For reminiscences of Fellini as a young boy in Rimini, written by the person who becomes the model for the protagonist of *Amarcord*, see Luigi "Titta" Benzi, *Patachédi: Gli amarcord di una vita all'insegna della grande amicizia con Federico Fellini* (Rimini: Guaraldi Editore, 1995).

4. In *Contemporary Italian Filmmaking: Strategies of Subversion* (Toronto: University of Toronto Press, 1995), Manuela Gieri discusses the relationship between Rome and the provinces in Fellini's work and draws a parallel to the relationship between Sicily and Rome in the works of Luigi Pirandello (one of the major aesthetic influences upon Fellini).

5. See this suggestion in my earlier work, *The Cinema of Federico Fellini* (Princeton: Princeton University Press, 1992), p. 328, which notes the direct links from Gambettola to Gelsomina to Ivo.

6. See ibid., p. 158, for a photograph of this particular dream sketch.

7. See Lietta Tornabuoni, ed., *Federico Fellini*, with a foreword by Martin Scorsese (New York: Rizzoli, 1995), pp. 347–82; Italian edition, *Federico Fellini* (Milan: Rizzoli, 1994). The show was held during 20 January–26 March 1995.

8. For numerous examples of Za's art, see Luigi Lambertini, *Nino Za: il caricaturista degli anni '30* (Bologna: Edizioni Bora, 1982).

9. Federico Fellini, *Comments on Film* (Fresno: California State University, 1988), ed. Giovanni Grazzini, trans. Joseph Henry (from *Intervista sul cinema* [Rome: Laterza, 1983]), p. 48.

10. Federico Fellini, "Comic-strip Heros," in *Fellini on Fellini*, pp. 140–1. For important discussions of Fellini's debt to the comic strips, see either Italo Calvino, "The Autobiography of a Spectator," or Oreste del Buono, "From Happy Hooligan to Giudizio, by Way of Little Nemo," both in Bondanella and Degli-Esposti, eds., *Perspectives on Federico Fellini*, pp. 25–30 and 31–4. Vincenzo Mollica's *Fellini: parole e disegni* (Turin: Einaudi, 2000) (English edition: *Fellini: Words and Drawings*, trans. Nina Marino [Welland, Ont.: Soleil Publishing, 2001]) is an important discussion of Fellini's relationship to cartoons. See also a number of Mollica-edited publications on cartoons and Fellini, including: *Fellini sognatore: omaggio all'arte di Federico Fellini* (Florence: Editori del grifo, 1992); *Il grifo (speciale Oscar Fellini) 3*, no. 22 (March 1993); *Scenari: il fumetto e il cinema di Fellini* (Montepulciano: Editori del grifo, 1984); and *Viaggio a Tulum: disegni di Milo Manara da un soggetto di Federico Fellini per un film da fare* (Montepulciano: Editori del grifo, 1991).

11. For a discussion of this phase of Fellini's career, see Tullio Kezich's fundamental biography, *Fellini* (Milan: Camunia Editrice, 1987), pp. 39–79. For a recent reproduction of the writings and drawings of Fellini for *Marc'-Aurelio*, see Lamberto Antonelli and Gabriele Paolini, eds., *Attalo e Fellini al "Marc'Aurelio": Scritti e disegni* (Rome: Napoleone, 1995). Important analyses of Fellini's early career may also be found in the following: Bondanella, *Cinema of Federico Fellini* (chaps. 1–2); Françoise Pieri, *Federico Fellini conteur et humoriste 1939–1942* (Perpignan: Éditions Jean Vigo, 2000); Gianfranco Angelucci, ed., *Federico Fellini da Rimini a Roma 1937–1947: Atti del convegno di studi e testimonianze Rimini, 31 ottobre*

1997 (Rimini: Pietroneno Capitani Editore, 1998); and Massimiliano Filippini and Vittorio Ferorelli, eds., *Federico Fellini autore di testi: Dal "Marc'Aurelio" a "Luci del Varietà" (1939–1950)* (Bologna: Quaderni IBC, 1999).

12. Gianfranco Angelucci, "Federico, Kafka, Pasqualino e la soubrette ammaliatrice," in Rossella Caruso and Giuseppe Casetti, eds., *"Il mio amico Pasqualino": Federico Fellini 1937–1947* (Rome: Il museo del louvre, 1997), pp. 11–13. Former Director of Rimini's Fondazione Federico Fellini, a group dedicated to the study of Fellini's life and art, Angelucci is one of Italy's most perceptive students of Fellini's cinema, was, for many years, Fellini's close collaborator, and coauthored the script of Fellini's penultimate feature film, *Intervista*. For a 1997 reprint of Fellini's first book (one of the first of many initiatives sponsored by the Fondazione), see *Il mio amico Pasqualino di Federico* (Rome: Edizioni dell'ippocampo, n.d. [probably 1942]; rpt. Rimini: Edizione della Fondazione Federico Fellini, 1997).

13. A reproduction of this drawing also appears in Bondanella, *Cinema of Federico Fellini*, p. 13.

14. For Guido Celano's account of this African adventure (and his claim that Fellini also scripted the film shot in Africa), see Francesco Savio, *Cinecittà anni trenta: parlano 116 protagonisti del secondo cinema italiano (1930–1943)*, ed. Tullio Kezich, 3 vols. (Rome: Bulzoni Editori, 1979), I: 304. Kezich, *Fellini* (p. 126), maintains that Fellini's first work behind the camera took place during the Florentine episode of *Paisan* when Fellini substituted briefly for Roberto Rossellini.

15. For a discussion of the birth of neorealism and its cinematic heritage, see Peter Bondanella, *Italian Cinema: From Neorealism to the Present*, 3d rev. ed. (New York: Continuum, 2001); Millicent Marcus, *Italian Cinema in the Light of Neorealism* (Princeton: Princeton University Press, 1986); and P. Adams Sitney, *Vital Crises in Italian Cinema: Iconography, Stylistics, Politics* (Austin: University of Texas Press, 1995). For Rossellini's part in the birth of neorealism, see Peter Bondanella, *The Films of Roberto Rossellini* (New York: Cambridge University Press, 1993).

16. See Ellen Draper, "'Controversy Has Probably Destroyed Forever the Context': *The Miracle* and Movie Censorship in America in the Fifties," *The Velvet Light Trap* 25 (1990): 69–79.

17. For Fellini's memories of his days with Lux, see Alberto Farassino and Tatti Sanguineti, eds., *Lux Film: Esthétique et système d'un studio italien* (Locarno: Éditions du Festival international du Film de Locarno, 1984), pp. 284–5.

18. See Bondanella, *Cinema of Federico Fellini* (chap. 3). For English scripts of these three early works, see Federico Fellini, *Early Screenplays: "Vari-*

ety Lights" and "The White Sheik" (New York: Grossman, 1971); and *Three Screenplays: "I vitelloni," "Il bidone," "The Temptations of Dr. Antonio"* (New York: Grossman, 1970). Published Italian scripts are listed in the Bibliography.

19. For a detailed discussion of this question, as well as an English version of the unshot script, see Federico Fellini, *"Moraldo in the City" & "A Journey with Anita,"* ed. and trans. John C. Stubbs (Urbana: University of Illinois Press, 1983).

20. Cited in Federico Fellini, *Federico Fellini's "Juliet of the Spirits,"* ed. Tullio Kezich (New York: Orion Press, 1965), p. 30.

21. For the script and a number of important articles about the making of *La strada* and its meaning, see Federico Fellini, *"La strada": Federico Fellini, Director,* ed. and trans. Peter Bondanella and Manuela Gieri (New Brunswick, N.J.: Rutgers University Press, 1987).

22. For the English script of *Il bidone,* see Fellini, *Three Screenplays.* For a journal devoted to the making of this film, see Dominique Delouche, "Journal d'un bidoniste," in Geneviève Agel, *Les chemins de Fellini* (Paris: Éditions du Cerf, 1956), pp. 98–157.

23. Cited in Tullio Kezich, *Su "La dolce vita" con Federico Fellini: Giorno per giorno la storia di un film che ha fatto epoca* (Venice: Marsilio Editori, 1996), p. 41. Kezich's indispensable diary of the making of this major work contains a wealth of interesting details about Fellini's creative methods at this stage of his career.

24. Scripts of *Le tentazioni del dottor Antonio* must be read with care since they frequently omit changes made in the final cut of the completed film. See Federico Fellini, *"8½" di Federico Fellini,* ed. Camilla Cederna (Bologna: Cappelli, 1965), pp. 165–90 (with text printed as an appendix to this more famous work); in English, see Fellini, *Three Screenplays,* pp. 253–88.

25. For details about this work as well as a script, see Liliana Betti, Ornella Volta, and Bernardino Zapponi, eds., *"Tre passi nel delirio" di F. Fellini, L. Malle, R. Vadim* (Bologna: Cappelli, 1968).

26. For a posthumous edition of this screenplay, see Federico Fellini, *Il viaggio di G. Mastorna* (Milan: Bompiani, 1995).

27. For a detailed discussion of Fellini's contribution to Roman mythology and imagery in the modern world, see my study *The Eternal City: Roman Images in the Modern World* (Chapel Hill: University of North Carolina Press, 1987).

28. For Greer's extremely persuasive and provocative defense of Fellini's film and the positive image of women she believes exists in his cinema, see Germaine Greer, "Fellinissimo," in Bondanella and Degli-Esposti, eds., *Perspectives on Federico Fellini,* pp. 225–39.

29. Federico Fellini, *Fare un film* (Milan: Einaudi, 1980).

30. For a brief history of Fellini's relationship to advertising, see my essay "Fellini e la Grande Tentatrice – Breve storia: dai maccheroncini Pop, alla Pasta Barilla al Banco di Roma," in Paolo Fabbri and Mario Guaraldi, eds., *Mystfest 1997: Mistici & Miraggi* (Milan: Mondadori, 1997), pp. 239–65. This catalog of the 1997 Mystfest Film Festival contains the papers presented at a symposium on Fellini and advertising, including essays by Millicent Marcus, Cristina Degli-Esposti, Manuela Gieri, Alberto Abruzzese, Sergio Brancato, and Marco Bertozzi.

31. For details, see Albino Ivardi Ganapini and Giancarlo Gonizzi, eds., *Barilla: cento anni di pubblicità e comunicazione* (Parma: Archivio Storico Barilla, 1994).

32. For a book devoted to this important series of commercials, see the collection of photographs shot on their set and published for the Fondazione Federico Fellini in Rimini, Italy: Gianfranco Angelucci, ed., *Gli ultimi sogni di Fellini* (Rimini: Pietroneno Capitani Editore, 1997).

Chapter 2. *La strada:* The Cinema of Poetry and the Road beyond Neorealism

1. Leo Longanesi, a journalist who supposedly invented the infamous slogan "Mussolini is always right," wrote in 1933 in an essay entitled "The Glass Eye": "We should make films that are extremely simple and spare in staging without using artificial sets – films that are shot as much as possible from reality. In fact, realism is precisely what is lacking in our films. It is necessary to go right out into the street, to take the movie camera into the streets, the courtyards, the barracks, and the train-stations. To make a natural and logical Italian film, it would be enough to go out in the street, to stop anywhere at all and observe what happens during a half hour with attentive eyes and with no preconceptions about style" (cited by Adriano Aprà and Patrizia Pistagnesi, eds., *The Fabulous Thirties: Italian Cinema 1929–1944* [Milan: Electra, 1979], p. 50). A comparison of this call for a Fascist realism with the more famous manifestos for a postwar realism written by Cesare Zavattini will show that both Longanesi and Zavattini are speaking about exactly the same kind of cinema. For Zavattini's often-quoted statement, "A Thesis on Neo-Realism," see David Overbey, ed., *Springtime in Italy: A Reader on Neo-Realism* (Hamden, Conn.: Shoestring Press, 1978), pp. 67–78.

2. Italo Calvino, preface to *The Path to the Nest of Spiders*, trans. Archibald Colquhoun (New York: Ecco Press, 1976), p. vii. I treat the parallel move beyond neorealism in film and literature in "Beyond Neorealism: Calvino, Fellini and Fantasy," *Michigan Romance Studies 16* (1996): 103–20.

3. André Bazin, *What Is Cinema? Vol. II*, ed. and trans. Hugh Gray (Berkeley: University of California Press, 1971), p. 51.

4. Roberto Rossellini, "An Interview with *Cahiers du Cinéma*," in Roberto Rossellini, *My Method: Writings & Interviews*, Adriano Aprà, ed. (New York: Marsilio, 1992), pp. 47–57, at 48.

5. Roberto Rossellini, "I Am Not the Father of Neorealism," in ibid., pp. 44–6, at 44.

6. André Bazin is absolutely correct in using this term to refer to critics such as Aristarco and others in Italy: "I do not believe I am falsifying its meaning by interpreting it as their substitution for socialist realism, whose theoretical and practical barrenness unfortunately does not need to be demonstrated." See Bazin, "*La strada*," in Federico Fellini, "*La strada*": *Federico Fellini, Director*, ed. and trans. Peter Bondanella and Manuela Gieri (New Brunswick, N.J.: Rutgers University Press, 1987), pp. 199–203, at 200.

7. Michelangelo Antonioni, "Colloquio con Michelangelo Antonioni," in Pierre Leprohoun, *Michelangelo Antonioni: An Introduction* (New York: Simon & Schuster, 1963), pp. 48–9, 89–90 (the original interview first appeared in 1958); another and slightly different version of the same ideas may be found in Michelangelo Antonioni, "A Talk with Michelangelo Antonioni on His Work," in *The Architecture of Vision: Writings & Interviews on Cinema*, eds. Carlo di Carlo and Giorgio Tinazzi (New York: Marsilio, 1996), pp. 22–3 (this statement dates from 1961).

8. Antonioni, "Talk with Michelangelo Antonioni," p. 23.

9. Millicent Marcus, "Fellini's *La strada*: Transcending Neorealism," in Peter Bondanella and Cristina Degli-Esposti, eds., *Perspectives on Federico Fellini* (New York: G. K. Hall/Maxwell Macmillan Intl., 1993), pp. 87–99, at 89.

10. Federico Fellini, *Fellini on Fellini*, ed. Anna Keel and Christian Strich, trans. Isabel Quigley (New York: Da Capo Press, 1996; rpt. of the original English edition [London: Eyre Methuen, 1976]), p. 52.

11. Ibid., p. 57.

12. Cited from Geneviève Agel, *Les chemins de Fellini* (Paris: Éditions du Cerf, 1956), pp. 128–9 (author's translation).

13. For a detailed discussion of Fellini's interest in cartoons, see Peter Bondanella, *The Cinema of Federico Fellini* (Princeton: Princeton University Press, 1992), chap. 1.

14. Federico Fellini, "The Genesis of *La strada*," in "*La strada*": *Federico Fellini, Director*, pp. 181–4, at 181–2.

15. Ibid., p. 183.

16. Ibid.

17. The Italian script for *La strada* may be consulted in "*I vitelloni*" *e* "*La strada*" (Milan: Longanesi, 1989). However, it is not an accurate account

of the final work and does not contain a number of major revisions that became part of the completed film during shooting and editing. In fact, very few of the published Fellini scripts in Italian are continuity scripts based upon the final cut. *"La strada": Federico Fellini, Director,* is an accurate continuity script in English yet also reprints a number of variants. In citing from *La strada,* I shall refer only to shot numbers taken from this continuity script, since it numbers each and every shot in the final version of the film.

18. Fellini, "Genesis of *La strada,*" p. 184.

19. Marcus, "Fellini's *La strada:* Transcending Neorealism," at 94.

20. For the translation of the passage from the original shooting script that was modified in the final version of the film, see note 9 in the section entitled "Notes on the Continuity Script" in Fellini, *"La strada": Federico Fellini, Director,* pp. 165–75, at 169–70.

21. The best treatment of Fellini's poetic imagery in his early films is to be found in Gilbert Salachas, "Fellini's Imagery from *Variety Lights* to *Juliet of the Spirits,*" in Bondanella, ed., *Federico Fellini: Essays in Criticism* (New York: Oxford University Press, 1978), pp. 205–19; another important discussion of Fellini's themes that takes into account works from his mature career may be found in Stuart Rosenthal, "Spectacle: Magnifying the Personal Vision," in ibid., pp. 289–302.

22. See Peter Harcourt, "The Secret Life of Federico Fellini," in ibid., pp. 239–53, at p. 242; rpt. in Fellini, *"La strada": Federico Fellini, Director,* pp. 239–52, at 242.

23. For a discussion of how Fellini came to invent the image of the horse, see Moraldo Rossi, "Fellini and the Phantom Horse" in Fellini, *"La strada": Federico Fellini, Director,* pp. 188–9.

24. Guido Aristarco, "Guido Aristarco Answers Fellini," in ibid., pp. 208–10, at 209.

25. Peter Harcourt, "Secret Life of Federico Fellini," p. 250–1; also in Bondanella, ed., *Federico Fellini: Essays in Criticism,* p. 251.

Chapter 3. *La dolce vita:* The Art Film Spectacular

1. For a collection of the letters exchanged between Simenon and Fellini after a friendship between them emerged from the Cannes experience, see *Carissimo Simenon – Mon Cher Fellini: Carteggio di Federico Fellini e Georges Simenon,* eds. Claude Gauteur and Silvia Sager (Milan: Adelphi Edizioni, 1998). Tullio Kezich, *Su "La dolce vita" con Federico Fellini: Giorno per giorno la storia di un film che ha fatto epoca* (Venice: Marsilio Editori, 1996), provides a diary of the making of the film. For the Italian script, see Federico Fellini, *La dolce vita* (Milan: Garzanti, 1981), a large section of which (pp. 161–220) contains an appendix reprinting many of

the scandalized, negative, or hysterical reactions against the film; an abbreviated English version is published in Federico Fellini, *La dolce vita,* trans. Oscar DeLiso and Bernard Shir-Cliff (New York: Ballantine, 1961). For a photographic history of the infamous paparazzi, the photographers whose very name is derived from Fellini's film, see Andrea Nemiz, *Vita, dolce vita* (Rome: Network Edizioni, 1983); for hundreds of beautiful photographs shot on the set of the film, see Gianfranco Angelucci, ed., *"La dolce vita": un film di Federico Fellini* (Rome: Editalia, 1989).

2. The figure is given in American billions. The box-office success of *La dolce vita* is discussed by Tullio Kezich in *Fellini* (Milan: Camunia Editrice, 1987), pp. 292–3.

3. John Baxter, *Fellini* (New York: St. Martin's, 1993), p. 164, reports that Fellini received fifty thousand dollars in cash plus a gold watch from his producer, Angelo Rizzoli.

4. See Paul Ginsborg's *A History of Contemporary Italy: Society and Politics 1943–1988* (New York: Penguin, 1990), especially chap. 7 ("The 'Economic Miracle,' Rural Exodus and Social Transformation, 1958–1963"), to which I am indebted for his excellent discussion of the rapid social and economic changes that took place while *La dolce vita* was being made and that eventually came to be symbolized by the film itself.

5. Fellini, *La dolce vita* (Italian ed.), p. 206, reports a letter published by the Vatican newspaper *L'Osservatore Romano* on 5 March 1960 that calls attention to the fact that a number of the most famous scenes in the film could be grounds for prosecution under this law. It must also be recorded that not all Catholics or priests rejected the film. Padre Angelo Arpa, a Jesuit who had befriended Fellini and had assisted him when he ran into censorship problems with *Le notti di Cabiria,* recounts the history of his relationship with Fellini concerning the film in *"La dolce vita": cronaca di una passione* (Naples: Parresía Editori, 1996).

6. For information on the Montesi Case, see Baxter, *Fellini,* pp. 143–4.

7. For a history of this phenomenon, see Hank Kaufman and Gene Lerner, *Hollywood sul Tevere* (Milan: Sperling & Kupfer Editori, 1982).

8. See Nemiz, *Vita, dolce vita,* for a collection of the most famous of the paparazzi photographs from the period.

9. The influence of Dante in *La dolce vita* is perceptively treated in John Welle's "Fellini's Use of Dante in *La dolce vita,*" rpt. in Peter Bondanella and Cristina Degli-Esposti, eds., *Perspectives on Federico Fellini* (New York: G. K. Hall/Maxwell Macmillan Intl., 1993), pp. 110–18. Fellini's indebtedness to Dante is also treated by Barbara Lewalski in "Federico Fellini's *Purgatory,*" *Massachusetts Review* 5 (1964): 567–73, rpt. in Bondanella, ed., *Federico Fellini: Essays in Criticism* (New York: Oxford University Press, 1978), pp. 113–20. Jacqueline Risset, the French translator of Dante and also a Fellini scholar, discusses the link between Dante

and Fellini in "Appunti II: Fellini e Dante" in *L'incantatore: Scritti su Fellini* (Milan: Libri Scheiwiller, 1994), pp. 89–95.

10. Pier Paolo Pasolini, "The Catholic Irrationalism of Fellini," *Film Criticism* 9, no. 1 (Fall 1984): 63–73; rpt. in Bondanella and Degli-Esposti, eds., *Perspectives on Federico Fellini*, pp. 101–9, at 106, 107.

11. Cited by Suzanne Budgen in *Fellini* (London: British Film Institute, 1966), p. 99.

12. Cited from *The New Yorker* (30 October 1965, p. 66) by Robert Richardson in "Waste Lands: The Breakdown of Order," rpt. in Bondanella, ed., *Federico Fellini: Essays in Criticism*, pp. 103–12, at 104.

13. Cited in Tullio Kezich, *Il dolce cinema* (Milan: Bompiani, 1978), p. 25 (author's translation).

14. Stuart Rosenthal, "Spectacle: Magnifying the Personal Vision," in Bondanella, ed., *Federico Fellini: Essays in Criticism*, pp. 289–302, at 300.

15. Federico Fellini, *Fellini on Fellini*, ed. Anna Keel and Christian Strich, trans. Isabel Quigley (New York: Da Capo Press, 1996; rpt. of the original English edition [London: Eyre Methuen, 1976]), p. 157.

16. Federico Fellini, *Comments on Film* (Fresno: California State University, 1988), ed. Giovanni Grazzini, trans. Joseph Henry (from *Intervista sul cinema* [Rome: Laterza, 1983]), p. 136.

17. Ibid., pp. 132–3.

18. Federico Fellini, *Un regista a Cinecittà* (Milan: Mondadori, 1988), p. 50 (author's translation).

19. Fellini, *La dolce vita* (English ed.), p. 36. All English dialogue is cited from this edition.

20. Ibid., p. 53.

21. Ibid., p. 75.

22. Martelli discusses this in Franca Faldini and Goffredo Fofi, eds., *L'avventurosa storia del cinema italiano raccontata dai suoi protagonisti 1960–1969* (Milan: Feltrinelli, 1981), pp. 10–11.

23. See Gherardi's comments in ibid., p. 12.

24. Stefano Masi and Enrico Lancia, *Italian Movie Goddesses: Over 80 of the Greatest Women in Italian Cinema* (Rome: Gremese, 1997), p. 120. This book is an indispensable history of postwar Italian actresses, especially interesting for the history of the phenomenon of the *maggiorata* or buxom actress that became so important in the period.

25. See Nemiz, *Vita, dolce vita*, for the photographs.

26. Masi and Lancia, *Italian Movie Goddesses*, p. 120.

27. See Barthélemy Amengual, "Fin d'itinéraire: du 'côté de chez Lumière' au 'côté de chez Méliès,'" *Études cinématographiques 127–30* (1981): 81–111, for the complete exposition of this perspective on Fellini's entire career.

Chapter 4. 8½: The Celebration of Artistic Creativity

1. Federico Fellini, *Fellini on Fellini*, ed. Anna Keel and Christian Strich, trans. Isabel Quigley (New York: Da Capo Press, 1996; rpt. of the original English edition [London: Eyre Methuen, 1976]), p. 147.

2. For a discussion of Fellini and Bernhard, see Tullio Kezich's *Fellini* (Milan: Camunia Editrice, 1987), pp. 302–7; for a more general discussion of Jung in Italian culture, see Alberto Carotenuto, *Jung e la cultura italiana* (Rome: Astrolabio, 1977). Peter Bondanella, *The Cinema of Federico Fellini* (Princeton: Princeton University Press, 1992), contains photographs of a number of Fellini's dream sketches.

3. Gideon Bachmann, "A Guest in My Own Dreams: An Interview with Federico Fellini, " *Film Quarterly* 47, no. 3 (1994): 2–15, at p. 7.

4. Barthélemy Amengual, "Une Mythologie fertile: *Mamma Puttana*," in Gilles Ciment, ed., *Federico Fellini* (Paris: Éditions Rivages, 1988), pp. 32–9, at 34.

5. Federico Fellini, *Comments on Film* (Fresno: California State University, 1988), ed. Giovanni Grazzini, trans. Joseph Henry (from *Intervista sul cinema* [Rome: Laterza, 1983]), p. 162.

6. There are a number of important books and articles devoted to the script and the filming of 8½. Two discussions of the film's shooting exist: Deena Boyer, *The Two Hundred Days of "8½"* (New York: Garland, 1978); and Camilla Cederna, "La bella confusione," in Federico Fellini, *"8½" di Federico Fellini*, ed. Cederna (Bologna: Cappelli, 1965), pp. 15–85. Two guides to analyzing the film exist in English: Ted Perry, *Filmguide to "8½"* (Bloomington: Indiana University Press, 1975); and Albert E. Benderson, *Critical Approaches to Federico Fellini's "8½"* (New York: Arno Press, 1974). The Italian script containing Cederna's essay is not a continuity script, since it presents the discarded ending of the film as its finale. As is the case with *La strada*, the most reliable continuity script available is in English: Federico Fellini, *"8½": Federico Fellini, Director*, ed. and trans. Charles Affron (New Brunswick: Rutgers University Press, 1987). References to 8½ will be made to this script by shot number rather than page number, as was the practice in the chapter on *La strada*.

7. Cited in Fellini, *"8½": Federico Fellini, Director*, p. 238.

8. Fellini, *Fellini on Fellini*, p. 52.

9. For a photograph of the note, see Federico Fellini, *Un regista a Cinecittà* (Milan: Mondadori, 1988), p. 50.

10. Ted Perry makes this important observation in *Filmguide to "8½,"* p. 21.

11. Donald Costello, *Fellini's Road* (Notre Dame: University of Notre Dame Press, 1983), pp. 83–8.

12. Fellini, *"8½": Federico Fellini, Director*, pp. 130, 132 (shots 460, 469).

Chapter 5. *Amarcord:* Nostalgia and Politics

1. Federico Fellini, *Comments on Film* (Fresno: California State University, 1988), ed. Giovanni Grazzini, trans. Joseph Henry (from *Intervista sul cinema* [Rome: Laterza, 1983]), p. 15.
2. Ibid., pp. 179–80.
3. Cited in Franca Faldini and Goffredo Fofi, eds., *L'avventurosa storia del cinema italiana raccontata dai suoi protagonisti 1960–1969* (Milan: Feltrinelli, 1981), p. 275 (author's translation).
4. Federico Fellini, *Fellini on Fellini*, ed. Anna Keel and Christian Strich, trans. Isabel Quigley (New York: Da Capo Press, 1996; rpt. of the original English edition [London: Eyre Methuen, 1976]), p. 151.
5. Ibid., pp. 157–8.
6. Federico Fellini to Gian Luigi Rondi, cited from the press book of *Amarcord* distributed by Roger Corman and New World Pictures when the film was first screened in the United States, p. 18 (author's private collection). This important statement should be read together with the fundamental interview Fellini has given on the film, entitled "*Amarcord:* The Fascism within Us," in Peter Bondanella, ed., *Federico Fellini: Essays in Criticism* (New York: Oxford University Press, 1978), pp. 20–6.
7. Fellini, *Fellini on Fellini*, p. 151.
8. For a survey of such theories, see A. J. Gregor, *Interpretations of Fascism* (Morristown, N.J.: General Learning Press, 1974); or Renzo De Felice, *Interpretations of Fascism* (Cambridge, Mass.: Harvard University Press, 1977).
9. For an English version of the script and a discussion of how two of Fellini's unshot scripts relate to his other films, including *La dolce vita* and *Amarcord*, see Federico Fellini, "*Moraldo in the City*" & "*A Journey with Anita*," ed. and trans. John C. Stubbs (Urbana: University of Illinois Press, 1983), especially pp. 167–70.
10. See Luigi "Titta" Benzi, *Patachédi: Gli amarcord di una vita all'insegna della grande amicizia con Federico Fellini* (Rimini: Guaraldi Editore, 1995), as well as several other works on Rimini and Fellini, mentioned in note 3 to Chapter 1.
11. Fellini, "*Amarcord:* The Fascism within Us," pp. 21–2.
12. Ibid., p. 21.
13. Federico Fellini to Gian Luigi Rondi, cited from the press book of *Amarcord* distributed by Roger Corman and New World Pictures when the film was first screened in the United States, p. 17 (author's private collection).
14. Ibid., p. 18.
15. See Millicent Marcus, "Fellini's *Amarcord*: Film as Memory," *Quarterly Review of Film Studies* 2, no. 4 (1977): 418–25, at 423.
16. Fellini, "*Amarcord:* The Fascism within Us," p. 20.

17. Cited from the subtitles to the restored version of *Amarcord* available on DVD and laser disc (Criterion Collection) or videocassette (Home Vision), translated by Gianfranco Angelucci and Peter Bondanella. The previously distributed dubbed version of *Amarcord* on videocassette is to be avoided at all costs, due to its completely unreliable translation of the original text, which is filled with dialect expressions and off-color phrases not rendered by the dubbed English. All subsequent citations from the sound track of this film will be taken directly from the DVD subtitles. For the Italian script of this particular passage, changed in important instances in the final version of the film, see *Il film "Amarcord" di Federico Fellini*, eds. Gianfranco Angelucci and Liliana Betti (Bologna: Cappelli, 1974), p. 199.
18. Ibid.
19. Federico Fellini, *Fare un film* (Milan: Einaudi, 1980), p. 41 (author's translation).
20. Fellini, "*Amarcord:* The Fascism within Us," p. 24.
21. Fellini, *Comments on Film*, p. 39.
22. Fellini, *Fellini on Fellini*, p. 49.

Chapter 6. *Intervista:* A Summation of a Cinematic Career

1. Federico Fellini, *Block-notes di un regista* (Milan: Longanesi, 1988), p. 69.
2. Cited by Dario Zanelli in *Nel mondo di Federico* (Turin: Nuova Edizioni ERI RAI, 1987), p. 14 (author's translation).
3. Cited by ibid., p. 17 (author's translation).
4. For a detailed comparison of *Intervista* and *Block-notes di un regista*, see my *The Cinema of Federico Fellini* (Princeton: Princeton University Press, 1992), pp. 206–7.
5. See Frank Burke's *Fellini's Films: From Postwar to Postmodern* (New York: Twayne, 1996), p. 276.
6. For this point, see Cristina Degli-Esposti's "Federico Fellini's *Intervista* or the Neo-Baroque Creativity of the Analysand on Screen," *Italica* 73, no. 2 (1996): 157–72, at 168. While American critics tend to see the concept "postmodern" as a novelty, Italian critics such as Umberto Eco and Omar Calabrese (not to mention Ernst Curtius) more correctly view postmodernity as a perennial form of neobaroque style. Thus, critics for years have remarked on Fellini's "baroque" style, and it is not surprising that his later works should also reflect postmodern tendencies as well.
7. Fellini, *Block-notes di un regista*, pp. 78, 79–80 (author's translation).
8. Burke, *Fellini's Films*, p. 277. Burke's reading of *Intervista* is quite convincing in its argument that Fellini's film embodies a number of postmodernist techniques of narration. However, his use of postcolonial theory to argue that Fellini presents a postcolonial image of Cinecittà and the figure of the film director, merely because the trip to the studio includes the fig-

ure of a Fascist *gerarca* (who is mercilessly satirized), represents exactly the kind of injudicious application of contemporary film theory to works lacking even the most basic concern with such questions that has made much recent writing on the cinema so disconnected from common sense. If there were ever a director less concerned with the issues that characterize postcolonial theory than Federico Fellini, I would not know how to name him or her. Moreover, contrary to Burke's view of Fellini in this book, which is based upon the premise that Fellini *must* be linked to contemporary film theory to have relevance, such connections merely serve to obscure Fellini's authentic artistic intentions, many (but not all) of which contradict postmodern notions about authorship in particular, even while they may well seem to embrace postmodern ideas about representation, mimesis, and simulation.

9. Federico Fellini, *Comments on Film* (Fresno: California State University, 1988), ed. Giovanni Grazzini, trans. Joseph Henry (from *Intervista sul cinema* [Rome: Laterza, 1983]), pp. 207–8.

10. Federico Fellini, *Ginger e Fred*, ed. Mino Guerrini (Milan: Longanesi, 1986), p. 76 (author's translation).

11. Fellini, *Comments on Film*, p. 102.

12. Typescript of *Real Dreams: Into the Dark with Federico Fellini*, BBC Television Script (1987), p. 13.

13. Federico Fellini, *Fellini on Fellini*, ed. Anna Keel and Christian Strich, trans. Isabel Quigley (New York: Da Capo Press, 1996; rpt. of the original English edition [London: Eyre Methuen, 1976]), p. 120. This is a statement Fellini has repeated throughout his career.

14. Fellini, *Block-notes di un regista*, p. 62 (author's translation).

15. Umberto Eco, *The Name of the Rose, Including the Author's Postscript*, trans. William Weaver (San Diego: Harcourt, 1994), pp. 530–1.

16. The anecdote is reported in Tullio Kezich's *Fellini* (Milan: Camunia Editrice, 1987), p. 276, where the producer is identified as Angelo Rizzoli, producer of *La dolce vita*.

17. Federico Fellini, *"8½": Federico Fellini, Director*, ed. and trans. Charles Affron (New Brunswick: Rutgers University Press, 1987), p. 39 (shot 20).

18. Fellini, *Block-notes di un regista*, p. 182 (author's translation).

19. Fellini, "Fellini on Television," in Bondanella, ed., *Federico Fellini: Essays in Criticism* (New York: Oxford University Press, 1978), pp. 11–16, at 14.

Selected Bibliography on Federico Fellini

The critical literature on Fellini in a number of languages represents an imposing mass of material. Because of the length of any comprehensive Fellini bibliography, this Selected Bibliography on Federico Fellini has been limited to the major books and scripts, with few articles, reviews, or interviews. For a critical guide through this material, see:

1. Peter Bondanella, "Recent Work on Italian Cinema." *Journal of Modern Italian Studies 1*, no. 1 (1995): 101–23; and
2. Peter Bondanella and Cristina Degli-Esposti, "Federico Fellini: A Brief Overview of the Critical Literature," in Peter Bondanella and Cristina Degli-Esposti, eds., *Perspectives on Federico Fellini* (New York: G. K. Hall / Maxwell Macmillan Intl., 1993), pp. 3–21.

This anthology of critical essays and an earlier such collection – Peter Bondanella, ed., *Federico Fellini: Essays in Criticism* (New York: Oxford University Press, 1978) – provide the reader with the most important work written on Fellini since the appearance of his first films. Tullio Kezich's *Fellini* (Milan: Camunia, 1987) is the fundamental biography of Fellini, although in English the reader may consult Hollis Alpert, *Fellini: A Life* (New York: Atheneum, 1986) and John Baxter, *Fellini* (New York: St. Martin's, 1993) with profit. Two invaluable Internet sites for information on Fellini may also be consulted:

1. the Internet Movie Data Base (www.imdb.com); and
2. the official site of the Federico Fellini Foundation, located in Rimini, Italy (www.netlab.it/fellini/fondazio.htm).

Agel, Geneviève. *Les chemins de Fellini*. Paris: Éditions du Cerf, 1956.

Alpert, Hollis. *Fellini: A Life*. New York: Atheneum, 1986.

Angelucci, Gianfranco. *"La dolce vita": un film di Federico Fellini*. Rome: Editalia, 1989.

  Gli ultimi sogni di Fellini. Rimini: Pietroneno Capitani Editore, 1997.

  ed. *Federico Fellini da Rimini a Roma 1937–1947: Atti del convegno di studi e testimonianze Rimini, 31 ottobre 1997*. Rimini: Pietroneno Capitani Editore, 1998.

Antonelli, Lamberto, and Gabriele Paolini, eds. *Attalo e Fellini al "Marc'Aurelio": Scritti e disegni*. Rome: Napoleone, 1995.

Arpa, Padre Angelo. *"La dolce vita": cronaca di una passione*. Naples: Parresía Editori, 1996.

  Fellini: persona e personaggio. Naples: Parresía Editori, 1996.

Bachmann, Gideon. "A Guest in My Own Dreams: An Interview with Federico Fellini." *Film Quarterly* 47, no. 3 (1994): 2–15.

Baxter, John. *Fellini*. New York: St. Martin's, 1993.

Bazin, André. *Bazin at Work: Major Essays & Reviews from the Forties & Fifties*. Ed. Bert Cardullo. Trans. Alain Piette and Bert Cardullo. New York: Routledge, 1977 [contains essays on Italian cinema not included in the volume *What Is Cinema? Vol. II* below].

  Qu'est-ce que le cinéma? – IV. Une esthétique de la Réalité: le néo-réalisme. Paris: Éditions du Cerf, 1962.

  What Is Cinema? Vol. II. Ed. and trans. Hugh Gray. Berkeley: University of California Press, 1971 [contains many of the essays in the French edition].

Benderson, Albert E. *Critical Approaches to Federico Fellini's "8½."* New York: Arno Press, 1974.

Benevelli, Elio. *Analisi di una messa in scena: Freud e Lacan nel "Casanova" di Fellini*. Bari: Dedali Libri, 1979.

Benzi, Luigi "Titta." *Patachédi: Gli amarcord di una vita all'insegna della grande amicizia con Federico Fellini*. Rimini: Guaraldi Editore, 1995.

Betti, Liliana. *Fellini: An Intimate Portrait*. Trans. Joachim Neugroschel. Boston: Little, Brown, 1979.

  Io e Fellini [Ma sei sicuro che non ci siano gli indiani?]. Milan: Archinto, 2000.

  ed. *Federico A. C.: disegni per il "Satyricon" di Federico Fellini*. Milan: Edizioni Libri, 1970.

Betti, Liliana, and Gianfranco Angelucci, eds. *Casanova rendez-vous con Federico Fellini*. Milan: Bompiani, 1975.

Betti, Liliana, and Oreste Del Buono, eds. *Federcord: disegni per "Amarcord" di Federico Fellini*. Milan: Edizioni Libri, 1974.

Bìspurri, Ennio. *Federico Fellini: il sentimento latino della vita*. Rome: Editrice Il Ventaglio, 1981.

Boledi, Luigi, and Raffaele De Berti, eds. *"Luci del Varietà": pagine scelte*. Milan: Il Castoro, 1999.

Bondanella, Peter. "*Amarcord:* Fellini and Politics." *Cinéaste 19*, no. 1 (1992): 36–43, 32.

"Beyond Neorealism: Calvino, Fellini and Fantasy." *Michigan Romance Studies 16* (1996): 103–20.

The Cinema of Federico Fellini. "Foreword" by Federico Fellini. Princeton: Princeton University Press, 1992. Italian edition with a new preface by the author: *Il cinema di Federico Fellini.* Rimini: Guaraldi Editore, 1994.

The Eternal City: Roman Images in the Modern World. Chapel Hill: University of North Carolina Press, 1987.

Italian Cinema: From Neorealism to the Present. 3d rev. ed. New York: Continuum, 2001.

"Recent Work on Italian Cinema." *Journal of Modern Italian Studies 1*, no. 1 (1995): 101–23.

ed. *Federico Fellini: Essays in Criticism.* New York: Oxford University Press, 1978.

Bondanella, Peter, and Cristina Degli-Esposti, eds. *Perspectives on Federico Fellini.* New York: G. K. Hall/Maxwell Macmillan Intl., 1993.

Borin, Fabrizio. *Federico Fellini.* Rome: Gremese, 1999.

Boyer, Deena. *The Two Hundred Days of "8½."* New York: Garland, 1978.

Brunetta, Gian Piero. *Storia del cinema italiano.* 4 vols. Rome: Editori Riuniti, 1993. Vol. I, *Il cinema muto 1895–1929;* vol. II, *Il cinema del regime 1929–1945;* vol. III, *Dal neorealismo al miracolo economico 1945–1959;* vol. IV, *Dal miracolo economico agli anni novanta 1960–1993.*

Storia del cinema mondiale. 4 volumes. Turin: Einaudi, 1999–.

Budgen, Suzanne. *Fellini.* London: British Film Institute, 1966.

Burke, Frank. *Federico Fellini: "Variety Lights" to "La dolce vita."* Boston: Twayne, 1984.

Fellini's Films: From Postwar to Postmodern. New York: Twayne, 1996.

Caruso, Rossella, and Giuseppe Casetti, eds. *"Il mio amico Pasqualino": Federico Fellini 1937–1947.* Rome: Il museo del louvre, 1997.

Chandler, Charlotte. *I, Fellini.* New York: Random House, 1995. Italian edition: *Federico Fellini.* Milan: Rizzoli, 1995. French edition: *Moi, Fellini: Treize ans de confidences.* Paris: Éditions Robert Laffont, 1994.

Cianfarani, Carmine, ed. *Federico Fellini: Leone d'Oro, Venezia 1985.* Rome: ANICA, 1985 [catalog of Fellini retrospective at 1985 Venice Film Festival].

Ciment, Gilles, ed. *Federico Fellini.* Paris: Éditions Rivages, 1988 [anthology of articles published by French journal *Positif*].

Cirio, Rita. *Il mestiere di regista: intervista con Federico Fellini.* Milan: Garzanti, 1994.

Collet, Jean. *La création selon Fellini.* Paris: José Corti, 1990.

Costello, Donald. *Fellini's Road.* Notre Dame, Ind.: University of Notre Dame Press, 1983.

de Miro, Ester, and Mario Guaraldi, eds. *Fellini della memoria*. Florence: La Casa Usher, 1983 [catalog for the 1983 Fellini retrospective at Rimini].

De Santi, Pier Marco. *I disegni di Fellini*. Rome: Laterza, 1982.

De Santi, Pier Marco, and Raffaele Monti, eds. *Saggi e documenti sopra "Il Casanova" di Federico Fellini*. Pisa: Quaderni dell'Istituto di storia dell'arte dell'Università di Pisa, 1978.

Estève, Michel, ed. *Federico Fellini: aux sources de l'imaginaire*. Paris: Études Cinématographiques, nos. 127–130, 1981.

——— ed. *Federico Fellini: "8½."* Paris: Études Cinématographiques, nos. 28–9, 1963.

Fabbri, Paolo, and Mario Guaraldi, eds. *Mystfest 1997: Mistici & Miraggi*. Milan: Mondadori, 1997.

Faldini, Franca, and Goffredo Fofi, eds. *L'avventurosa storia del cinema italiano raccontata dai suoi protagonisti 1935–1959*. Milan: Feltrinelli, 1979.

——— *L'avventurosa storia del cinema italiano raccontata dai suoi protagonisti 1960–1969*. Milan: Feltrinelli, 1981.

——— *Il cinema italiano d'oggi 1970–1984 raccontato dai suoi protagonisti*. Milan: Mondadori, 1984.

Fantuzzi, Virgilio. *Il vero Fellini*. Rome: Ave Editrice, 1994.

Farassino, Alberto, and Tatti Sanguineti. *Lux Film: Esthétique et système d'un studio italien*. Locarno: Éditions du Festival international du Film de Locarno, 1984.

Fava, Claudio G., and Aldo Viganò. *I film di Federico Fellini*. 2d ed. Rome: Gremese Editore, 1987. English edition: *The Films of Federico Fellini*. Trans. Shula Curto. Secaucus, N.J.: Citadel Press, 1985 [translation of 1st Italian edition of 1981].

Federico Fellini. CD-ROM. Rome: Progetti Museali Editori/ENEL, 1995.

Fellini, Federico. *Block-notes di un regista*. Milan: Longanesi, 1988.

——— *Casanova*. Ed. Federico Fellini and Bernardino Zapponi. Turin: Einaudi, 1977.

——— *La città delle donne*. Milan: Garzanti, 1980.

——— *I clowns*. Ed. Renzo Renzi. Bologna: Cappelli, 1970.

——— *La dolce vita*. Trans. Oscar DeLiso and Bernard Shir-Cliff. New York: Ballantine, 1961.

——— *La dolce vita*. Milan: Garzanti, 1981.

——— *Early Screenplays: "Variety Lights" and "The White Sheik."* New York: Grossman, 1971.

——— *"8½": Federico Fellini, Director*. Ed. and trans. Charles Affron. New Brunswick, N.J.: Rutgers University Press, 1987.

——— *E la nave va*. Ed. Federico Fellini and Tonino Guerra. Milan: Longanesi, 1983.

——— *Fare un film*. Turin: Einaudi, 1980.

Federico Fellini's "Juliet of the Spirits." Ed. Tullio Kezich. New York: Orion Press, 1965.

Fellini on Fellini. Ed. Anna Keel and Christian Strich. Trans. Isabel Quigley. New York: Da Capo Press, 1996. Rpt. of original English edition, London: Eyre Methuen, 1976.

Fellini Satyricon. Ed. Dario Zanelli. Bologna: Cappelli, 1969.

Fellini's Casanova. Ed. Bernardino Zapponi. New York: Dell, 1977.

Fellini's Satyricon. Ed. Dario Zanelli. New York: Ballantine, 1970.

Fellini TV: "Blocknotes di un regista" / "I clowns." Ed. Renzo Renzi. Bologna: Cappelli, 1972.

Il film "Amarcord" di Federico Fellini. Ed. Gianfranco Angelucci and Liliana Betti. Bologna: Cappelli, 1974.

Ginger e Fred. Ed. Mino Guerrini. Milan: Longanesi, 1986.

Giulietta. Genoa: Il melangolo, 1994.

Intervista sul cinema. Ed. Giovanni Grazzini. Rome: Laterza, 1983. English edition: *Comments on Film.* Trans. Joseph Henry. Fresno: California State University, 1988.

La mia Rimini. Bologna: Cappelli, 1987; original edition 1967.

Il mio amico Pasqualino di Federico. Rome: Edizioni dell'ippocampo, n.d. (probably 1942). Rpt. Rimini: Edizione della Fondazione Federico Fellini, 1997.

"Moraldo in the City" & "A Journey with Anita." Ed. and trans. John C. Stubbs. Urbana: University of Illinois Press, 1983 [unrealized screenplays].

Le notti di Cabiria. Milan: Garzanti, 1981.

"8½" di Federico Fellini. Ed. Camilla Cederna. Bologna: Cappelli, 1965.

Il primo Fellini: "Lo sceicco bianco," "I vitelloni," "La strada," "Il bidone." Ed. Renzo Renzi. Bologna: Cappelli, 1969.

Prova d'orchestra. Milan: Garzanti, 1980.

Quattro film. Intro. by Italo Calvino. Turin: Einaudi, 1974.

Raccontando di me: Conversazioni con Costanzo Costantini. Rome: Editori Riuniti, 1996. English edition: *Fellini on Fellini.* Ed. Costanzo Costantini. Trans. Sohrab Sorooshian. London: Faber & Faber, and San Diego: Harvest, 1995.

Un regista a Cinecittà. Milan: Mondadori, 1988.

"Roma" di Federico Fellini. Ed. Bernardino Zapponi. Bologna: Cappelli, 1972.

Lo sceicco bianco. Milan: Garzanti, 1980.

La strada. Ed. François-Regis Bastide, Juliette Caputo, and Chris Marker. Paris: Éditions du Seuil, 1955.

La strada. L'Avant-Scène du Cinéma 102 (April 1970): 7–51.

"La strada": Federico Fellini, Director. Ed. Peter Bondanella and Manuela Gieri. New Brunswick, N.J.: Rutgers University Press, 1987.

"La strada": sceneggiatura originale di Federico Fellini e Tullio Pinelli. Rome: Edizioni Bianco e Nero, 1955.

Three Screenplays: "I vitelloni," "Il bidone," "The Temptations of Dr. Antonio." New York: Grossman, 1970.

"Tre passi nel delirio" di F. Fellini, L. Malle, R. Vadim. Ed. Liliana Betti, Ornella Volta, and Bernardino Zapponi. Bologna: Cappelli, 1968.

Il viaggio di G. Mastorna. Milan: Bompiani, 1995.

"I vitelloni" e "La strada." Milan: Longanesi, 1989.

La voce della luna. Turin: Einaudi, 1990.

La voce della luna. Ed. Lietta Tornabuoni. Florence: La Nuova Italia, 1990.

Fellini, Federico, and Georges Simenon. *Carissimo Simenon – Mon cher Fellini: carteggio di Federico Fellini e Georges Simenon.* Ed. Claude Gauteur and Silvia Sager. Milan: Adelphi Edizioni, 1998.

Filippini, Massimiliano, and Vittorio Ferorelli, eds. *Federico Fellini autore di testi: Dal "Marc'Aurelio" a "Luci del Varietà" (1939–1950).* Bologna: Quaderni IBC, 1999.

Fofi, Goffredo, and Gianni Volpi, eds. *Federico Fellini: l'arte della visione.* Grugliasco: Tipografia Torinese, 1993.

Gallagher, Tag. *The Adventures of Roberto Rossellini: His Life and Films.* New York: Da Capo Press, 1998.

Giacci, Vittorio, ed. *La voce della luce: Federico Fellini.* Rome: Progetti Museali Editore, 1995.

Gieri, Manuela. *Contemporary Italian Filmmaking: Strategies of Subversion.* Toronto: University of Toronto Press, 1995.

Gori, Gianfranco Miro, ed. *Rimini e le cinéma: images, cinéastes, histoires.* Exh. cat. Paris: Éditions du Centre Georges Pompidou, 1989.

Grau, Jordi. *Fellini desde Barcelona.* Barcelona: Ambit Servicios Editoriales, 1985.

Hughes, Eileen Lanouette. *On the Set of "Fellini Satyricon": A Behind-the-Scenes Diary.* New York: Morrow, 1971.

James, Clive. "Mondo Fellini." *The New Yorker 70,* no. 5 (21 March 1994): 154–65.

Kauffmann, Stanley. "Fellini, Farewell." *The New Republic* (31 January 1994): 28–30.

Kaufman, Hank, and Gene Lerner. *Hollywood sul Tevere.* Milan: Sperling & Kupfer Editori, 1982.

Ketcham, Charles B. *Federico Fellini: The Search for a New Mythology.* New York: Paulist Press, 1976.

Kezich, Tullio. *Il dolce cinema.* Milan: Bompiani, 1978.

Fellini. Milan: Camunia Editrice, 1987.

Fellini del giorno dopo con un alfabetiere felliniano. Rimini: Editori Guaraldi, 1996.

Giulietta Masina. Bologna: Cappelli, 1991.

Su "La dolce vita" con Federico Fellini: Giorno per giorno la storia di un film che ha fatto epoca. Venice: Marsilio Editori, 1996.

Laura, Ernesto G., ed. *Tutti i film di Venezia 1932–1984.* 2 vols. Venice: La Biennale, 1985.

Marcus, Millicent. *After Fellini: National Cinema in the Postmodern Age.* Baltimore: Johns Hopkins University Press, 2001.

——— . *Filmmaking by the Book: Italian Cinema and Literary Adaptation.* Baltimore: Johns Hopkins University Press, 1993.

——— . *Italian Film in the Light of Neorealism.* Princeton: Princeton University Press, 1986.

Mariotti, Franco, ed. *Cinecittà tra cronaca e storia 1937–1989.* 2 vols. Rome: Presidenza del Consiglio dei Ministri, 1989.

Mingozzi, Gianfranco, ed. *Dolce dolce vita: immagini da un set di Federico Fellini.* Casalecchio di Reno: Giorgio Menna Editore, 1999.

Mollica, Vincenzo. *Fellini: parole e disegni.* Turin: Einaudi, 2000. English edition: *Fellini: Words and Drawings.* Trans. Nina Marino. Welland, Ont.: Soleil Publishing, 2001.

——— . ed. *Fellini sognatore: omaggio all'arte di Federico Fellini.* Florence: Editori del grifo, 1992.

——— . ed. *Il grifo (speciale Oscar Fellini) 3,* no. 22 (March 1993).

——— . ed. *Scenari: il fumetto e il cinema di Fellini.* Montepulciano: Editori del grifo, 1984.

——— . ed. *Viaggio a Tulum: disegni di Milo Manara da un soggetto di Federico Fellini per un film da fare.* Montepulciano: Editori del grifo, 1991.

Monti, Fiorella, and Elisabetta Zanzi, eds. *Fellini e dintorni: Cinema e psicoanalisi.* Cesena: Il Ponte Vecchio, 1996.

Monti, Raffaele, ed. *Bottega Fellini: "La città delle donne": progetto, lavorazione, film.* Rome: De Luca, 1981.

Monti, Raffaele, and Pier Marco De Santi, eds. *L'invenzione consapevole: disegni e materiali di Federico Fellini per il film "E la nave va."* Florence: Artificio, 1984.

Murray, Edward. *Fellini the Artist.* 2d ed. New York: Frederick Ungar, 1985.

Pecori, Franco. *Federico Fellini.* Florence: La Nuova Italia, 1974.

Perry, Ted. *Filmguide to "8½."* Bloomington: Indiana University Press, 1975.

Pieri, Françoise. *Federico Fellini conteur et humoriste 1939–1942.* Perpignan: Éditions Jean Vigo, 2000.

Prats, A. J. *The Autonomous Image: Cinematic Narration & Humanism.* Lexington: University Press of Kentucky, 1981.

Price, Barbara Anne, and Theodore Price. *Federico Fellini: An Annotated International Bibliography.* Metuchen, N.J.: Scarecrow Press, 1978.

Provenzano, Roberto C. *Invito al cinema di Fellini.* Milan: Mursia, 1995.

Rondi, Brunello. *Il cinema di Fellini.* Rome: Edizioni di Bianco e Nero, 1965.

Rosenthal, Stuart. *The Cinema of Federico Fellini*. New York: A. S. Barnes, 1976.

Salachas, Gilbert. *Federico Fellini: An Investigation into His Films and Philosophy*. Trans. Rosalie Siegel. New York: Crown, 1969 [translation of original French edition, *Federico Fellini*. Paris: Éditions Seghers, 1963. Cinema d'aujourd'hui no. 13.]

Solmi, Angelo. *Fellini*. London: Merlin Press, 1967.

Strich, Christian, ed. *Fellini's Faces*. New York: Holt, Rinehart & Winston, 1982.

———. ed. *Fellini's Films: The Four Hundred Most Memorable Stills from Federico Fellini's Fifteen and a Half Films*. New York: Putnam's, 1977.

Stubbs, John C. *Federico Fellini: A Guide to References and Resources*. Boston: G. K. Hall, 1978.

Tatò, Francesco, ed. *The Stuff Dreams Are Made Of: The Films of Marcello Mastroianni*. Rome: Marchesi Garfiche Editoriali, 1998.

Tornabuoni, Lietta, ed. *Federico Fellini*. Foreword by Martin Scorsese. New York: Rizzoli, 1995. English edition of *Federico Fellini*. Rome: Cinecittà International, 1994.

Tutto Fellini su CD-ROM. CD-ROM. Rome: Editoria Elettronica Editel/Ente dello spettacolo, 1994.

Verdone, Mario. *Federico Fellini*. Florence: La Nuova Italia, 1994.

Zanelli, Dario. *L'inferno immaginario di Federico Fellini: cose dette da F. F. a proposito de "Il Viaggio di G. Mastorna."* Ravenna: Guaraldi Editore, 1995.

———. *Nel mondo di Federico*. Preface by Federico Fellini. Turin: Nuova Edizioni ERI RAI, 1987.

Zanzotto, Andrea. *Filò: per il "Casanova" di Fellini*. Milan: Mondadori, 1988. English translation: *Peasants Wake for Fellini's "Casanova" and Other Poems*. Ed. and trans. John P. Welle and Ruth Feldman. Urbana: University of Illinois Press, 1997.

Zapponi, Bernardino. *Il mio Fellini*. Venice: Marsilio Editori, 1995.

A Fellini Filmography

Principal Credits

N.B.: An attempt has been made to distinguish bona fide English-language release titles (*Like This*) from mere translations [Like This]. Dates given are those of first release.

I. Films Scripted for Other Directors

Imputato alzatevi! ([Defendant, On Your Feet!] 1939)
DIRECTOR: Mario Mattoli
SCRIPT : Vittorio Metz, Mario Mattoli (Fellini not credited)

Lo vedi come sei? ([Do You See How You Are?] 1939)
DIRECTOR: Mario Mattoli
SCRIPT: Vittorio Metz, Steno, and Mario Mattoli (Fellini not credited)

Non me lo dire! ([Don't Tell Me!] 1940)
DIRECTOR: Mario Mattoli
SCRIPT: Vittorio Metz, Marcello Marchesi, Steno, Mario Mattoli (Fellini not credited)

Il pirata sono io ([The Pirate Is Me] 1940)
DIRECTOR: Mario Mattoli
SCRIPT: Vittorio Metz, Steno, Marcello Marchesi, Mario Mattoli (Fellini not credited)

Avanti c'è posto ([There's Room Up Ahead] 1942)
DIRECTOR: Mario Bonnard
SCRIPT: Aldo Fabrizi, Cesare Zavattini, Piero Tellini, Federico Fellini (listed as scriptwriter in film's registration documents but not credited by film's titles)

Documento Z-3 ([Document Z-3] 1942)
DIRECTOR: Alfredo Guarini
SCRIPT: Sandro De Feo, Alfredo Guarini, Ercoli Patti (Fellini not credited)

Campo de' fiori ([Campo de' Fiori Square], *Peddler and the Lady,* 1943)
DIRECTOR: Mario Bonnard
SCRIPT: Aldo Fabrizi, Federico Fellini, Piero Tellini, Mario Bonnard

L'ultima carrozzella ([The Last Carriage] 1943)
DIRECTOR: Mario Bonnard
SCRIPT: Aldo Fabrizi, Federico Fellini

Quarta pagina ([The Fourth Page] 1943)
DIRECTOR: Nicola Manzari
SCRIPT: Piero Tellini, Federico Fellini, Edoardo Anton, Ugo Betti, Nicola Manzari, Spiro Manzari, Giuseppe Marotta, Gianni Puccini, Steno, Cesare Zavattini (seven episodes, each scripted by different writers)

Chi l'ha visto? ([Who's Seen Him?] completed 1943; released 1945)
DIRECTOR: Goffredo Alessandrini
SCRIPT: Federico Fellini, Piero Tellini

Gli ultimi Tuareg ([The Last Tauregs], 1943)
DIRECTOR: Gino Talamo
SCRIPT: Federico Fellini and others (?) – film shot but never released

Apparizione ([Apparition] 1944)
DIRECTOR: Jean de Limur
SCRIPT: Piero Tellini, Lucio De Caro, Giuseppe Amato (Fellini not credited)

Tutta la città canta ([The Whole City Is Singing] 1945)
DIRECTOR: Riccardo Freda
SCRIPT: Vittorio Metz, Marcello Marchesi, Steno (Fellini not credited)

Roma, città aperta (*Open City,* a.k.a. *Rome, Open City,* 1945)
DIRECTOR: Roberto Rossellini
SCRIPT: Alberto Consiglio, Sergio Amidei, Roberto Rossellini, Federico Fellini

Paisà (*Paisan,* 1946)
DIRECTOR: Roberto Rossellini
SCRIPT: Sergio Amidei, Klaus Mann, Alfred Hayes, Marcello Pagliero, Roberto Rossellini, Federico Fellini

Il delitto di Giovanni Episcopo ([The Crime of Giovanni Episcopo], *Flesh Will Surrender,* 1947)
DIRECTOR: Alberto Lattuada
SCRIPT: Piero Tellini, Suso Cecchi D'Amico, Aldo Fabrizi, Alberto Lattuada, Federico Fellini

Il passatore (A Bullet for Stefano, 1947)
DIRECTOR: Duilio Coletti
SCRIPT: Tullio Pinelli, Federico Fellini

Senza pietà (Without Pity, 1948)
DIRECTOR: Alberto Lattuada
SCRIPT: Tullio Pinelli, Alberto Lattuada, Federico Fellini, Ettore Maria Margadonna

Il miracolo (The Miracle, 1948), part II of *L'amore (The Ways of Love,* 1948)
DIRECTOR: Roberto Rossellini
SCRIPT: Federico Fellini, Tullio Pinelli, Roberto Rossellini

Il mulino del Po (The Mill on the Po, 1949)
DIRECTOR: Alberto Lattuada
SCRIPT: Riccardo Bacchelli, Mario Bonfantini, Luigi Comencini, Carlo Musso, Sergio Romano, Alberto Lattuada, Tullio Pinelli, Federico Fellini

In nome della legge (In the Name of the Law, 1949)
DIRECTOR: Pietro Germi
SCRIPT: Aldo Bizzarri, Pietro Germi, Giuseppe Mangione, Mario Monicelli, Tullio Pinelli, Federico Fellini

Francesco, giullare di dio (The Flowers of Saint Francis; The Adventures of St. Francis of Assisi; a.k.a. *Francis, God's Jester,* 1950)
DIRECTOR: Roberto Rossellini
SCRIPT: Roberto Rossellini, Federico Fellini, with the assistance of Father Félix Morlion and Father Antonio Lisandrini

Il cammino della speranza (The Path of Hope, 1950)
DIRECTOR: Pietro Germi
SCRIPT: Pietro Germi, Tullio Pinelli, Federico Fellini

La città si difende ([The City Defends Itself], *Four Ways Out,* 1951)
DIRECTOR: Pietro Germi
SCRIPT: Pietro Germi, Tullio Pinelli, Giuseppe Mangione, Federico Fellini

Persiane chiuse (Behind Closed Shutters, 1951)
DIRECTOR: Luigi Comencini
SCRIPT: Tullio Pinelli, Federico Fellini

Europa '51 (The Greatest Love, 1952)
DIRECTOR: Roberto Rossellini
SCRIPT: Sandro De Feo, Roberto Rossellini, Mario Pannunzio, Ivo Perilli, Diego Fabbri, Antonio Pietrangeli, Brunello Rondi (Fellini not credited)

Il brigante di Tacca del Lupo ([The Bandit of Tacca del Lupo] 1952)
DIRECTOR: Pietro Germi
SCRIPT: Tullio Pinelli, Pietro Germi, Fausto Tozzi, Federico Fellini

Fortunella (1958)
DIRECTOR: Eduardo De Filippo
SCRIPT: Federico Fellini

Viaggio con Anita (*Lovers and Liars*, a.k.a. *Travels with Anita*, 1979)
DIRECTOR: Mario Monicelli
SCRIPT: Tullio Pinelli (Fellini not credited)

II. Films Directed by Federico Fellini

Luci del varietà (*Variety Lights*, a.k.a. *Lights of Variety*, 1950)
SCRIPT: Alberto Lattuada, Federico Fellini, Tullio Pinelli, Ennio Flaiano
PHOTOGRAPHY: Otello Martelli
MUSIC: Felice Lattuada
SET DESIGN: Aldo Buzzi
EDITING: Mario Bonotti
PRODUCER: Capitolium Film
CAST: Peppino De Filippo (Checco), Carlo Del Poggio (Liliana), Giulietta Masina (Melina), Johnny Kitzmiller (Johnny), Giulio Cali (Edison Will), Carlo Romano (Renzo), Folco Lulli (Conti)

Lo sceicco bianco (*The White Sheik*, 1952)
SCRIPT: Federico Fellini, Tullio Pinelli, Ennio Flaiano
PHOTOGRAPHY: Arturo Gallea
MUSIC: Nino Rota
SET DESIGN: Federico Fellini
EDITING: Rolando Benedetti
PRODUCER: Luigi Rovere
CAST: Brunella Bovo (Wanda Cavalli), Leopoldo Trieste (Ivan Cavalli), Alberto Sordi (Fernando Rivoli), Giulietta Masina (Cabiria), Fanny Marchiò (Marilena Velardi), Ernesto Almirante (*fotoromanzo* director), Ettore Margadonna (Ivan's uncle)

I vitelloni (a.k.a. *The Young and the Passionate; Spivs*, 1953)
SCRIPT: Federico Fellini, Tullio Pinelli, Ennio Flaiano
PHOTOGRAPHY: Otello Martelli
MUSIC: Nino Rota
SET DESIGN: Mario Chiari
EDITING: Rolando Benedetti
PRODUCER: Peg Films–Cité Films
CAST: Franco Interlenghi (Moraldo), Franco Fabrizi (Fausto), Alberto Sordi (Alberto), Leopoldo Trieste (Leopoldo), Riccardo Fellini (Riccardo), Eleonora Ruffo (Sandra), Jean Brochard (Fausto's father), Claude Farrell (Alberto's sister), Carlo Romano (Signor Michele), Enrico Viarisio (Sandra's father), Lida Baarova (Giulia), Arlette Sauvage (woman in the cinema)

Un'agenzia matrimoniale ([A Matrimonial Agency], 1953), one episode in *Amore in città* (*Love in the City*, 1953)
SCRIPT: Federico Fellini and Tullio Pinelli
PHOTOGRAPHY: Gianni di Venanzo
MUSIC: Mario Nascimbene
SET DESIGN: Gianni Polidori
EDITING: Eraldo da Roma
PRODUCER: Faro Films
CAST: Antonio Cifariello (journalist), Livia Venturini (Rossana)

La strada (1954)
SCRIPT: Federico Fellini, Tullio Pinelli, Ennio Flaiano
PHOTOGRAPHY: Otello Martelli
MUSIC: Nino Rota
SET DESIGN: Mario Ravasco
EDITING: Leo Catozzo
PRODUCER: Carlo Ponti and Dino De Laurentiis
CAST: Giulietta Masina (Gelsomina), Anthony Quinn (Zampanò), Richard Basehart (the Fool), Aldo Silvani (circus owner), Marcella Rovere (the widow), Livia Venturini (the nun)

Il bidone (*The Swindle,* 1955)
SCRIPT: Federico Fellini, Tullio Pinelli, Ennio Flaiano
PHOTOGRAPHY: Otello Martelli
MUSIC: Nino Rota
SET DESIGN: Dario Cecchi
EDITING: Mario Serandrei and Giuseppe Vari
PRODUCER: Titanus
CAST: Broderick Crawford (Augusto), Richard Basehart (Picasso), Franco Fabrizi (Roberto), Giulietta Masina (Iris), Lorella De Luca (Patrizia), Giacomo Gabrielli (Vargas), Sue Ellen Blake (Anna), Alberto De Amicis (Goffredo), Irena Cefaro (Marisa)

Le notti di Cabiria (*The Nights of Cabiria,* 1957)
SCRIPT: Federico Fellini, Tullio Pinelli, Ennio Flaiano with the collaboration of Pier Paolo Pasolini for dialogue
PHOTOGRAPHY: Aldo Tonti and Otello Martelli
MUSIC: Nino Rota
SET DESIGN: Piero Gherardi
EDITING: Leo Catozzo
PRODUCER: Dino De Laurentiis
CAST: Giulietta Masina (Cabiria), Amedeo Nazzari (the actor), François Périer (Oscar D'Onofrio), Aldo Silvani (hypnotist), Franca Marzi (Wanda), Dorian Gray (Jessy), Franco Fabrizi (Giorgio), Mario Passange (the cripple), Pina Gualandri (Matilda)

La dolce vita (1959)
SCRIPT: Federico Fellini, Tullio Pinelli, Ennio Flaiano, Brunello Rondi
PHOTOGRAPHY: Otello Martelli
MUSIC: Nino Rota
SET DESIGN: Piero Gherardi
EDITING: Leo Catozzo
PRODUCER: Riama Film–Pathé Consortium Cinéma
CAST: Marcello Mastroianni (Marcello Rubini), Anouk Aimée (Maddalena), Anita Ekberg (Sylvia), Walter Santesso (Paparazzo), Lex Barker (Robert), Yvonne Fourneaux (Emma), Alain Cuny (Steiner), Annibale Ninchi (Marcello's father), Polidor (clown), Nadia Gray (Nadia), Valeria Ciangottini (Paola), Magali Noël (Fanny), Alan Dijon (Frankie Stout), and numerous minor characters

Le tentazioni del dottor Antonio (*The Temptations of Doctor Antonio*, 1962), an episode in *Boccaccio '70* (*Boccaccio '70*, 1962)
SCRIPT: Federico Fellini, Tullio Pinelli, Ennio Flaiano
PHOTOGRAPHY: Otello Martelli
MUSIC: Nino Rota
SET DESIGN: Piero Zuffi
EDITING: Leo Catozzo
PRODUCER: Carlo Ponti and Antonio Cervi
CAST: Peppino De Filippo (Doctor Antonio Mazzuolo), Anita Ekberg (Anita), Donatella Della Nora (Mazzuolo's sister), Antonio Acqua (Commendatore La Pappa), Elenora Maggi (Cupid)

8 ½ (a.k.a. *Otto e mezzo*, 1963)
SCRIPT: Federico Fellini, Tullio Pinelli, Ennio Flaiano, Brunello Rondi
PHOTOGRAPHY: Gianni di Venanzo
MUSIC: Nino Rota
SET DESIGN: Piero Gherardi
EDITING: Leo Catozzo
PRODUCER: Angelo Rizzoli
CAST: Marcello Mastroianni (Guido Anselmi), Anouk Aimée (Luisa), Sandra Milo (Carla), Claudia Cardinale (Claudia), Rossella Falk (Rossella), Edra Gale (La Saraghina), Caterina Boratto (the Beautiful Unknown Woman), Madeleine Lebeau (the French actress), Barbara Steel (Gloria Morin), Mario Pisu (Mario Mezzabotta), Guido Alberti (Pace the producer), Jean Rougeul (Daumier the critic), Ian Dallas (Maurice the telepath), Tito Masini (the cardinal), Annibale Ninchi (Guido's father), Giuditta Rissone (Guido's mother), Yvonne Casadei (Jacqueline Bonbon), Marco Gemini (Guido as a schoolboy), Riccardo Guglielmi (Guido at farmhouse), plus numerous other minor characters

Giulietta degli spiriti (*Juliet of the Spirits*, 1965)
SCRIPT: Federico Fellini, Tullio Pinelli, Ennio Flaiano, Brunello Rondi
PHOTOGRAPHY: Gianni di Venanzo
MUSIC: Nino Rota

SET DESIGN: Piero Gherardi
EDITING: Ruggero Mastroianni
PRODUCER: Angelo Rizzoli
CAST: Giulietta Masina (Giulietta), Mario Pisu (Giorgio, Giulietta's husband), Sandra Milo (Susy/Iris/Fanny), Lou Gilbert (grandfather), Caterina Boratto (Giulietta's mother), Luisa Della Noce (Adele), Sylva Koscina (Sylva), Valentina Cortese (Val), Valeska Gert (Bhisma), Alberto Plebani (Lynx-Eyes, the private detective), José de Villalonga (José), Silvana Jachino (Dolores), Elena Fondra (Elena), and numerous minor characters

Toby Dammit (1968), an episode in *Tre passi nel delirio* (*Spirits of the Dead;* a.k.a. *Histoires Extraordinaires; Tales of Mystery and Imagination,* 1968)
SCRIPT: Federico Fellini, Bernardino Zapponi
PHOTOGRAPHY: Giuseppe Rotunno
MUSIC: Nino Rota
SET DESIGN: Piero Tosi
EDITING: Ruggero Mastroianni
PRODUCER: Les Films Marceau/Cocinor–P. E. A. Cinematografica
CAST: Terence Stamp (Toby Dammit), Salvo Randone (priest), Antonia Pietrosi (actress), Polidor (old actor), Marina Yaru (the devil as a young girl)

Block-notes di un regista (*Fellini: A Director's Notebook,* 1969)
SCRIPT: Federico Fellini
PHOTOGRAPHY: Pasquale De Santis
MUSIC: Nino Rota
SET DESIGN: Federico Fellini
EDITING: Ruggero Mastroianni
PRODUCER: NBC-TV and Peter Goldfarb
CAST: Federico Fellini, Giulietta Masina, Marcello Mastroianni, Marina Boratto, Caterina Boratto, Pasquale De Santis, Genius the Medium, and numerous nonprofessionals

Satyricon (*Fellini's Satyricon,* 1969)
SCRIPT: Federico Fellini, Bernardino Zapponi
PHOTOGRAPHY: Giuseppe Rotunno
MUSIC: Nino Rota
SET DESIGN: Danilo Donati
EDITING: Ruggero Mastroianni
PRODUCER: Alberto Grimaldi
CAST: Martin Potter (Encolpio), Hiram Keller (Ascilto), Max Born (Gitone), Mario Romagnoli (Trimalchione), Fanfulla (Vernacchio), Gordon Mitchell (robber), Alain Cuny (Lica), Joseph Wheeler (husband suicide), Lucia Bosè (wife suicide), Donyale Luna (Enotea), Salvo Randone (Eumolpo), Magali Noël (Fortunata), Hylette Adolphe (slave girl), Pasquale Baldassare (hermaphrodite), Luigi Montefiori (Minotaur), Gennaro Sabatino (ferryman), Marcello di Falco (Proconsul), Tanya Lopert (emperor)

I clowns (The Clowns, 1970)
SCRIPT: Federico Fellini, Bernardino Zapponi
PHOTOGRAPHY: Dario di Palma
MUSIC: Nino Rota
SET DESIGN: Danilo Donati
EDITING: Ruggero Mastroianni
PRODUCER: Federico Fellini, Ugo Guerra, Elio Scardamaglia
CAST: *Film crew* – Maya Morin, Lina Alberti, Gasperino, Alvaro Vitali; *French clowns* – Alex, Bario, Père Loriot, Ludo, Nino, Charlie Rivel; *Italian clowns* – Riccardo Billi, Fanfulla, Tino Scotti, Carlo Rizzo, Freddo Pistoni, the Colombaioni, Merli, Maggio, Valdemaro Bevilacqua, Janigro, Terzo, Vingelli, Fumagalli; *others as themselves* – Federico Fellini, Liana Orfei, Tristan Rémy, Anita Ekberg, Victoria Chaplin, Franco Migliorini, Baptiste, Pierre Etaix

Roma (Fellini's Roma, 1972)
SCRIPT: Federico Fellini, Bernardino Zapponi
PHOTOGRAPHY: Giuseppe Rotunno
MUSIC: Nino Rota
SET DESIGN: Danilo Donati
EDITING: Ruggero Mastroianni
PRODUCER: Turi Vasile
CAST: Peter Gonzales (young Fellini), Fiona Florence (beautiful prostitute), Pia De Doses (aristocratic princess), Alvaro Vitali (tap dancer), Libero Frissi, Mario Del Vago, Galliano Sbarra, Alfredo Adami (performers in music hall), Federico Fellini, Marcello Mastroianni, Gore Vidal, Anna Magnani, and Alberto Sordi as themselves

Amarcord (1973)
SCRIPT: Federico Fellini, Tonino Guerra
PHOTOGRAPHY: Giuseppe Rotunno
MUSIC: Nino Rota
SET DESIGN: Danilo Donati
EDITING: Ruggero Mastroianni
PRODUCER: Franco Cristaldi
CAST: Bruno Zanin (Titta), Pupella Maggio (Miranda, Titta's mother), Armando Brancia (Aurelio, Titta's father), Nando Orfei (Lallo, Il Pataca), Peppino Ianigro (Titta's grandfather), Ciccio Ingrassia (mad Uncle Teo), Magali Noël (Gradisca), Josiane Tanzilli (Volpina), Maria Antonietta Beluzzi (tobacconist), Gennaro Ombra (Biscein the liar), Aristide Caporale (Giudizio), Alvaro Vitali (Naso), Bruno Scagnetti (Ovo), Bruno Lenzi (Gigliozzi), Fernando de Felice (Ciccio), Donatella Gambini (Aldina), Franco Magno (Zeus the headmaster), Mauro Misul (philosophy teacher), Dina Adorni (math teacher), Francesco Maselli (physics teacher), Mario Silvestri (Italian teacher), Fides Stagni (art history teacher), Mario Liberati (owner of movie theater), Domenico Pertica (blind accordion player)

Il Casanova di Fellini (Fellini's Casanova, 1976)
SCRIPT: Federico Fellini, Bernardino Zapponi with lyrics by Andrea Zanzotto and Tonino Guerra
PHOTOGRAPHY: Giuseppe Rotunno
MUSIC: Nino Rota
SET DESIGN: Danilo Donati
EDITING: Ruggero Mastroianni
PRODUCER: Alberto Grimaldi and Universal–Fox–Gaumont–Titanus
CAST: Donald Sutherland (Casanova), Cicely Browne (Madame d'Urfé), Tina Aumont (Henriette), Margareth Clementi (Maddalena), Olimpia Carlisi (Isabella), Daniel Emilfork (Dubois), Sandy Allen (the giantess), Claretta Algrandi (Marcolina), Clarissa Roll (Annamaria), Marika Rivera (Astrodi), Adele Angela Lojodice (the mechanical doll), John Karlsen (Lord Talou), Mario Gagliardo (Righetto), Angelica Hansen (hunchbacked actress)

Prova d'orchestra (Orchestra Rehearsal, 1979)
SCRIPT: Federico Fellini, Brunello Rondi
PHOTOGRAPHY: Giuseppe Rotunno
MUSIC: Nino Rota
SET DESIGN: Dante Ferretti
EDITING: Ruggero Mastroianni
PRODUCER: Daime Cinematografica and RAI-TV, Albatros Produktion
CAST: Baldwin Baas (orchestra conductor), David Mauhsell (first violinist), Francesco Aluigi (second violinist), Angelica Hansen and Heinz Kreuger (violinists), Elisabeth Labi (pianist), Ronaldo Bonacchi (contrabassoon), Giovanni Javarone (tuba), Andy Miller (oboe), Umberto Zuanelli (copyist), Claudio Ciocca (union leader), Sibyl Mostert (flutist), Franco Mazzieri (trumpet player), Daniele Pagani (trombone player)

La città delle donne (City of Women, 1980)
SCRIPT: Federico Fellini, Bernardino Zapponi, Brunello Rondi
PHOTOGRAPHY: Giuseppe Rotunno
MUSIC: Luis Bacalov
SET DESIGN: Dante Ferretti
EDITING: Ruggero Mastroianni
PRODUCER: Opera Film Production and Gaumont
CAST: Marcello Mastroianni (Snàporaz), Anna Prucnal (Snàporaz's wife), Bernice Stegers (mysterious woman on the train), Ettore Manni (Katzone), Donatella Damiani and Rosaria Tafuri (the two *soubrettes*), Hélène Calzarelli, Dominique Labourier, Sylvie Mayer, Maïté Nahyr, Loredana Solfizi (feminists)

E la nave va (And the Ship Sails On, 1983)
SCRIPT: Federico Fellini, Tonino Guerra with opera lyrics by Andrea Zanzotto
PHOTOGRAPHY: Giuseppe Rotunno
MUSIC: Gianfranco Plenizio
SET DESIGN: Dante Ferretti

EDITING: Ruggero Mastroianni
PRODUCER: Franco Cristaldi, RAI-TV, Vides Produzione, Gaumont
CAST: Freddie Jones (Orlando), Barbara Jefford (Ildebranda Cuffari), Janet Suzman (Edmea Tetua), Vittorio Poletti (Aureliano Fuciletto), Peter Cellier (Sir Reginald Dongby), Norma West (Lady Violet Dongby), Pina Bausch (Princess), Pasquale Zito (Count of Bassano), Fiorenzo Serra (Grand Duke), Philip Locke (Prime Minister)

"Oh, che bel paesaggio!" ([Oh, What a Beautiful Landscape!], 1984) – a television commercial for Campari Bitter aperitif
SCRIPT: Federico Fellini
PHOTOGRAPHY: Ennio Guarnieri
MUSIC: Nicola Piovani
SET DESIGN: Dante Ferretti
EDITING: Ugo De Rossi
PRODUCER: Giulio Romieri, BRW
CAST: Vittorio Poletti, Silvia Dionisio, Antonella Barchiesi

"Alta Società" ([High Society], 1984) – a television commercial for Barilla rigatoni pasta
SCRIPT: Federico Fellini
PHOTOGRAPHY: Ennio Guarnieri.
MUSIC: Nino Rota, arranged by Nicola Piovani.
SET DESIGN: Danilo Dolci
EDITING: Ugo De Rossi and Anna Amedei
PRODUCER: Fabrizio Capucci, International Cbn
CAST: Greta Vaian; Maurizio Mauri

Ginger e Fred (*Ginger and Fred*, 1985)
SCRIPT: Federico Fellini, Tullio Pinelli, Tonino Guerra
PHOTOGRAPHY: Tonino Delli Colli
MUSIC: Nicola Piovani
SET DESIGN: Dante Ferretti
EDITING: Nino Baragli, Ugo De Rossi, Ruggero Mastroianni
PRODUCER: Alberti Grimaldi
CAST: Giulietta Masina (Amelia or "Ginger"), Marcello Mastroianni (Pippo or "Fred"), Franco Fabrizi (master of ceremonies of variety show), Frederick Ledenburg (admiral), Augusto Poderosi (transvestite), Jacque Henri Lartigue (priest), Toto Mignone (Toto), Luciano Lombardo (defrocked priest), and numerous minor figures

Intervista ([Interview], 1987)
SCRIPT: Federico Fellini, Gianfranco Angelucci
PHOTOGRAPHY: Tonino Delli Colli
MUSIC: Nicola Piovani

SET DESIGN: Danilo Donati
EDITING: Nino Baragli
PRODUCER: Ibrahim Moussa, Aljosha Productions, RAI-UNO
CAST: Sergio Rubini (journalist), Paola Liguori (movie star), Maurizio Mein (assistant director), Nadia Ottaviani (custodian of Cinecittà's archives), Anita Ekberg, Federico Fellini, Marcello Mastroianni, and a host of other members of the troupe as themselves

La voce della luna (*The Voice of the Moon,* 1990)
SCRIPT: Federico Fellini, Tullio Pinelli, Ermanno Cavazzoni
PHOTOGRAPHY: Tonino Delli Colli
MUSIC: Nicola Piovani
SET DESIGN: Dante Ferretti
EDITING: Nino Baragli
PRODUCER: Mario and Vittorio Cecchi Gori, RAI–UNO
CAST: Roberto Benigni (Ivo Salvini), Paolo Villaggio (Prefect Gonnella), Marisa Tomasi (Marisa), Nadia Ottaviani (Aldina Ferruzzi), Algelo Orlando (Nestore), Uta Schmidt (Ivo's grandmother), George Taylor (Marisa's lover), Susy Blady (Susy)

"Che brutte notti!" (1992) – three television commercials for the Banca di Roma entitled "Il sogno del 'déjeuner sur l'herbe'" [The Picnic Lunch Dream]; "Il sogno della galleria" [The Tunnel Dream]; and "Il sogno del leone in cantina" [The Dream of the Lion in the Cellar]
SCRIPT: Federico Fellini
PHOTOGRAPHY: Giuseppe Rotunno
MUSIC: Nicola Piovani
SET DESIGN: Antonello Geleng
EDITING: Nino Baragli
PRODUCER: Roberto Mannoni
CAST: Paolo Villaggio, Anna Falchi, Fernando Rey, Ellen Rossi Stuart

Additional Films Cited

All That Jazz, dir. Bob Fosse (USA, 20th C.–Fox/Columbia, 1979)

Le amiche (*The Girlfriends*), dir. Michelangelo Antonioni (Italy, Trionfalcine–Titanus, 1955)

L'avventura, dir. Michelangelo Antonioni (Cino del Duca/PCE/Lyre, Italy, 1960)

Barry Lyndon, dir. Stanley Kubrick (Great Britain, Hawk Films/Peregrine/Polaris, 1975)

Beau Geste, dir. William Wellman (USA, Paramount, 1939)

Ben-Hur, dir. William Wyler (USA, MGM, 1959)

Bronenosets Potemkin (*Battleship Potemkin*), dir. Sergei Eisenstein (Goskino, USSR, 1925 [theatrical release 1926])

Casablanca, dir. Michael Curtiz (USA, Warner Bros., 1942)

Ciao, Federico! Fellini Directs Satyricon, dir. Gideon Bachman (Victor Herbert, 1969)

Cleopatra, dir. Joseph L. Mankiewicz (USA–UK–Switzerland, 20th C.–Fox/MCL Films/Walwa, 1963)

Il conformista (*The Conformist*), dir. Bernardo Bertolucci (Italy–France–W. Germany, Mars/Marianne/Maran, 1970)

Cronaca di un amore (*Story of a Love Affair;* a.k.a *Chronicle of a Love*), dir. Michelangelo Antonioni (Italy, Villani Films, 1950)

Falling Down, dir. Joel Shumacher (USA–France, Alcor Films/Le Studio Canal+/Regency Enterprises/Warner Bros., 1993)

Giovanna d'Arco al rogo (*Joan of Arc at the Stake*), dir. Roberto Rossellini (Italy, Produzioni Cinemagrafiche Associate/Franco–London Film, 1955)

The Godfather, Francis Ford Coppola (USA, Paramount, 1972)

Gone with the Wind, dir. Victor Fleming [George Cukor et al., uncredited], prod. David O. Selznick (MGM/Selznick Intl. Pictures, 1939)

Il grido (*The Cry;* a.k.a. *The Outcry*), dir. Michelangelo Antonioni (Italy, Sp.A. Cinematografica/Robert Alexander, 1957)

Ladri di biciclette (*The Bicycle Thief;* a.k.a. *Bicycle Thieves*), dir. Vittorio De Sica (PDS–ENIC, Italy, 1948)

1900 (*Novecento;* a.k.a. *Nineteen Hundred*), dir. Bernardo Bertolucci (Italy–France–Germany, PEA/Artistes Associés/Artermis, 1976) (in two parts)

Nuovo Cinema Paradiso (*Cinema Paradiso*), dir. Giuseppe Tornatore (Cristaldi Film/Films Ariadne, Italy–France, 1988)

Pasqualino Settebellezze (*Seven Beauties*), dir. Lina Wertmüller (Italy, Medusa, 1976)

La paura (*Fear; Die Angst*), dir. Roberto Rossellini (Italy–Germany, Geiselgasteig/Ariston Film/Aniene Film [Munich], 1954) (rereleased as *Non credo più all'amore,* 1955)

The Purple Rose of Cairo, dir. Woody Allen (USA, Rollins–Joffe/Orion, 1985)

Riso amaro (*Bitter Rice*), dir. Giuseppe De Santis (Italy, DEG/Lux, 1948)

Sciuscià (*Shoeshine*), dir. Vittorio De Sica (Italy, Alfa Cinematografica, 1946)

Senso (*Wanton Countessa;* a.k.a. *Feeling;* English-language version, *The Wanton Countess*), dir. Luchino Visconti (Italy, Lux, 1954)

The Sheik, dir. George Melford (USA, Famous Players–Lasky, 1921)

Son of the Sheik, dir. George Fitzmaurice (USA, Paramount, 1926)

Stardust Memories, dir. Woody Allen (USA, Rollins–Joffe, 1980)

Stromboli, terra di dio (*Stromboli, Land of God*), dir. Roberto Rossellini (Italy, Be-Ro/RKO, completed 1949 [latter cut half an hour for UK/USA release]; released 1951)

Sweet Charity, dir. Bob Fosse (USA, Universal, 1969)

La terra trema[: Episodio del mare] (The Earth Trembles[: Episode of the Sea]), dir. Luchino Visconti (Universalia, Italy, 1948)

Umberto D., dir. Vittorio De Sica (Italy, Amato Film/De Sica/Rizzoli Film Sp.A., 1951)

L'uomo delle stelle (*The Star Maker;* a.k.a. *Starmaker; The Star Man*), dir. Giuseppe Tornatore (Italy, Vittorio & Rita Cecchi Gori, 1996)

Viaggio in Italia (*Voyage in Italy*; a.k.a. *Strangers; Journey to Italy; The Lonely Woman; Voyage to Italy*), dir. Roberto Rossellini (Italy, Italiafilm / Junior Film / Sveva Film, 1953)

I vinti (*The Vanquished*), dir. Michelangelo Antonioni (Italy, Film Costellazione, 1952)

La vita è bella (*Life Is Beautiful*), dir. Roberto Benigni (Melampo Cinematografica, 1997)

Index

Printed in the United States
56346LVS00006B/1-30